Ray Offenburger, CFP®

THE RETIREMENT PARADOX

Why Successful People Fail at Retirement

INFLUENTIAL ADVISOR
MEDIA

Published by **Influential Advisor Media**

www.influentialadvisormedia.com

ISBN Paperback 979-8-950583-14-8

ISBN Hardback 979-8-950583-15-5

ISBN Epub979-8-950583-16-2

First Edition: September, 2026

Printed in the United States of America

DISCLAIMER

The information in this book is educational only and reflects opinions, viewpoints, and analyses of Raymond Offenburger, which are subject to change any time without notice.

This book is not intended as legal or tax advice. Accordingly, any tax information provided herein is not intended or written to be used, and cannot be used, by any taxpayer for the purpose of avoiding penalties that may be imposed on the taxpayer. Any tax information was written to support the scenario(s) or matter(s) addressed and you should seek advice based on your particular circumstances from an independent tax advisor. The information in this book is not investment or securities advice and does not constitute an offer or solicitation of any kind.

Individuals should speak with a financial professional before making any investment decisions. All investing involves risk, including entire loss of principal invested.

The names of the clients have been changed to protect the identity of the client at the client's request. Roth IRA contributions may generally be withdrawn tax-free at any time. Earnings may generally be withdrawn income tax-free if the individual has held amounts in a Roth IRA for at least 5 years and the withdrawal is made after age 59 ½. If the withdrawal is made before the 5-year period and age 59 ½, income taxes and an additional 10 percent federal income tax penalty may apply. Other exceptions may apply.

An annuity is a long-term insurance contract issued by an insurance company designed to provide a retirement income stream for life. Once the contract principal is converted into an income stream, you will no longer have access to your principal as a lump sum. Terms, conditions, limitations and surrender charges may apply. For costs and complete details, contact your financial professional.

CONTENTS

INTRODUCTION

THE RETIREMENT MIRAGE

WHEN SUCCESS BECOMES YOUR BIGGEST OBSTACLE

I'll never forget the moment I met Sarah and Jim[1]. They sat across from me in my office with a stack of account statements that represented forty years of hard work.

Like most of my clients, they were W-2 employees who had done everything right. Sarah had spent thirty-five years as a lab technician at the local hospital; Jim had worked his way up to operations manager at a pharmaceutical company. Between their 401(k)s, IRAs, and savings, they had accumulated a significant nest egg.

"We finally hit the $2 million mark last year," Jim said, his voice tight with anxiety. "Everyone says that's the magic number for retirement. But we can't shake the feeling it's not enough." Sarah nodded, adding quietly, "We're afraid to replace our fifteen-year-old car. What if we need that money later?"

Here was a couple who had done everything by the book. They maxed out their 401(k)s every year, lived well below their means, and never carried debt. And it worked. They had more than $2 million saved up. But watching them sit there, afraid to replace their old car? That's when you realize something's broken. They were living like they had maybe half of what they'd saved. The same discipline that helped them save all that money was now keeping them from enjoying any of it.

I see this pattern so often, I've developed a phrase for it. *Don't sacrifice living well so you can die wealthy*. That's exactly what Sarah and Jim were doing, and maybe it's what you're doing, too.

You worked hard. You saved diligently. You followed all the advice. You contributed to your 401(k), paid off the mortgage, and built your nest egg.

Now retirement is here, or maybe it's just around the corner. But instead of feeling confident, you feel something else. Anxiety. Uncertainty. Doubt.

You're not alone. The very habits that made you a successful saver can become your biggest obstacles in retirement.

THE RETIREMENT PARADOX

Every year, I sit down with dozens of retirees and near-retirees just like Sarah and Jim. These are smart, successful people, including engineers, teachers, managers, and healthcare workers who spent careers building solid financial foundations. Yet something feels off.

Their accounts are scattered across three or four institutions. Their taxes are higher than they expected. They're afraid to spend the money they worked so hard to save. Their financial advisor doesn't talk to their CPA, and their attorney hasn't reviewed their will in a decade. Their adult children still rely on them financially. And while they're technically "retired," they haven't quite figured out what that's supposed to feel like.

During my career, I have noticed that the people who have been the best savers and feel the most prepared financially are often the least prepared emotionally and strategically for actually living in retirement.

MY WAKE-UP CALL

Let me be honest. I didn't always understand this, myself. When I first started meeting with retirees, I thought I had all the answers. Just get the numbers right, optimize the portfolio, and everyone would be happy. I couldn't have been more wrong. I soon learned that having a well-allocated investment portfolio is not the same as having a financial plan. The only certainty in retirement is that there will be uncertainty. The job of a financial plan is to prepare for that uncertainty.

No one can predict the future. We have educated guesses, but they're still guesses. What I do know is that we can plan and prepare for whatever is going to happen. That means whenever you need money, you should have a plan for where to get it from. You need to be ready and able to make a rational decision when you might think the sky is falling, and your world is falling apart. You don't want to make irrational decisions when it matters the most.

That's why I do what I do. I learned from helping real people.

I started getting calls from clients two or three years into retirement. The money was fine, but they weren't. They were anxious, disconnected, and struggling to find purpose. One client put it perfectly. "Ray, I've got the money to do anything, but I don't know what I'm supposed to do."

The issue is that most retirement advice focuses on accumulation or how to grow your money. But the game completely changes at retirement. Now it's about distribution, coordination, protection, and purpose. That's a whole different skill set, and most people and their financial advisors are unprepared for it.

That's why I developed my simple philosophy. Successful retirement requires the financial security to sleep well at night and a reason to wake up in the morning. Most financial advisors focus only on the first part. But what good is financial security if you're paralyzed by fear of spending what you've saved?

WHAT THIS BOOK IS REALLY ABOUT

This isn't another retirement guide filled with generic tips or market predictions. You won't find complicated formulas or academic theories here.

Instead, this is a wake-up call about the real reasons retirees fail . . . not because they ran out of money but because they never had a plan that brought everything together.

Retirement isn't a one-time event. It's a strategic, ongoing process that must evolve with your life, your health, your goals, and your family.

Yet too many people approach it as if all they need is a "balanced portfolio" and they're good to go. But investments are just one piece of the puzzle.

A real retirement plan answers questions like these.

- How do I coordinate withdrawals from all of these scattered accounts without triggering unnecessary taxes?
- When should I take Social Security to maximize my lifetime benefits?
- How do I shift from saving to spending without the constant anxiety?
- What happens to all of these accounts when I'm gone?
- How do I find purpose and connection beyond my paycheck?

By answering these questions, we are creating a roadmap for your retirement. It's not just a pile of money but a clear path showing you how to get from where you are today to where you want to be with all the turns, stops, and destinations marked along the way.

WHO SHOULD READ THIS BOOK?

If you see any part of yourself in Sarah and Jim's story, this book is for you.

Maybe you've got adult children who still need help from time to time, and you're torn between wanting to be generous and worrying about your own security. Or perhaps you're frustrated because your financial advisor says one thing, your tax professional says another, and your attorney hasn't looked at your documents in years. Nobody's talking to each other, and you're stuck in the middle trying to make sense of it all.

The bottom line is, if you want to stop living in fear of running out of money and start actually enjoying what you've worked so hard to save, then yes, this book is for you.

THE HIDDEN TRAPS AHEAD

Throughout this book, I'm going to show you the mistakes I see people making, and trust me, I've seen a lot. Some of these may resonate with you, making you think, "Oh, that's me." Others you might not even realize you are doing until you read them on the page.

In the pages ahead, we'll explore these traps.

- The "Safe Money" Trap: why playing it safe might be the riskiest strategy of all (I'll share why one client's CDs were actually costing her more than any market downturn would have);
- "Just in Case" Paralysis: the dangerous psychology of under-living in retirement (including my client who wouldn't spend $180 on a hotel when her AC broke in 95-degree heat);
- The Tax Time Bomb: when the government owns part of your retirement and why your heirs might pay the price (including how one widow's tax rate jumped from 12 percent to 22 percent one year after her husband passed away);

- Scattered Success: when multiple accounts across different institutions create multiple problems (like the client who walked into my office with a tote bag full of statements from eight different banks across three towns);
- The Social Security Filing Disaster: the mistakes that leave money on the table for life and can devastate a surviving spouse (including the client whose decision to file at sixty-two cost her over $200,000 in lifetime income);
- The Silent Partnership: what happens when only one spouse knows the plan (and you will meet the widow who discovered several new accounts months after her husband died and had no idea how to access any of them);
- Toxic Generosity: when helping your family financially backfires and threatens your own security (like the couple who gave $200,000 to their adult son over three years without realizing how much it was adding up);
- The Loneliness Trap: when financial security isn't enough for a fulfilling retirement (including the recently retired executive who told me, "I wake up, have my coffee, and then . . . nothing. I don't know what to do with myself");
- Legacy Lost: how poor planning hurts the people you love most (like the three siblings who sat in my office barely speaking to each other because their father never explained why he structured his estate the way he did).
- The Number That Really Matters: it's not how much you have; it's whether that money can create a reliable income for as long as you live (I'll show you why a couple with $850,000 might have fewer concerns than a couple with $2 million).

YOUR PATH TO CONFIDENCE

Each chapter takes you inside one of these traps. But more importantly, I'll help you avoid them using strategies I've developed while working with real people facing real retirement challenges.

I've learned that you don't need a magic number. You don't need to beat the market. You don't need complicated strategies that only work on paper.

What you need is clarity about where you are, confidence about where you're going, and a coordinated plan that actually works in real life.

You've worked too hard to spend retirement worried. It's time to move from anxiety to confidence, from fear to freedom. Let me show you how.

CHAPTER 1

THE "SAFE MONEY" TRAP: HOW PLAYING IT SAFE CAN RUIN YOUR RETIREMENT

"We just want to keep things safe."

I hear this phrase all the time, especially from smart, responsible people who've spent their lives making careful financial decisions. They don't want to chase hot stocks. They don't want to "gamble" their retirement. They'd rather stick to cash, CDs, short-term bonds, or a "balanced" portfolio that they are confident is conservative.

Playing it safe feels right. It feels responsible. But in retirement, appearances can be deceiving. Sometimes the safest-looking choice creates the riskiest outcome of running out of purchasing power precisely when you need it most. Playing it safe can hurt you more than help you.

In this chapter, we'll discuss why those "safe" investments might actually be putting your retirement at risk, the critical difference between what you can emotionally handle and what your money needs to do for you, and how to build real security, not just the illusion of it.

THE COMFORT OF CASH AND ITS HIDDEN COST

Ray's Rule #1

Safety isn't a steady account value.
Safety is steady purchasing power.

Let's talk about cash and CDs. These instruments feel safe because their value doesn't swing wildly with the market. They're FDIC-insured. They're simple to understand. You can see the interest accrue and know exactly what you'll get.

But the cost you can't see on a monthly statement is lost purchasing power. If inflation is 3 percent, and your CD earns 2 percent, you're moving backward in real life. You won't notice it in year one. However, you will really feel it in Year 15 if rates remain the same[2].

HISTORICAL PRICES OF COMMON ITEMS* According to the Bureau of Labor Statistics		
Item	**Price c. 1990**	**Price c. 2025**
Gallon of Milk	$2.19	$4.07
Loaf of Bread	$0.97	$2.78
Gallon of Gasoline	$1.22	$2.87
New Car	$15,500	$50,080
Median Home Price	$98,300	$415,200

When you were working, you likely weren't thinking about needing this money for twenty or thirty years. You were thinking five years out, maybe. But retirement? That could be twenty-five, even thirty-five years for some folks. That $500,000 in the bank? If it's still just $500,000 in twenty-five years, it's not going to buy nearly as much as it does today. You preserved a number and lost a lifestyle.

I've worked with many diligent savers who were so focused on living off the interest, never touching their principal, that they were significantly reducing what they were going to be able to do in retirement. The goal is noble; the math is unforgiving. There's no way that's keeping up with inflation. If your intention is only to spend that interest, then you're shooting yourself in the foot.

Retirees who "play it safe" often don't realize their money is slowly losing ground. It's like standing still on an escalator that's going down.

But here's what really worries me about this "safe money" approach . . .

THE HEALTHCARE WILD CARD

Many people think Medicare covers everything. It doesn't. Over a long retirement, out-of-pocket costs, long-term care, supplemental premiums, drug plans, and uncovered services (like dental and vision) can arrive unevenly and can create tens or even hundreds of thousands in unexpected bills over time.

If the bulk of your nest egg sits in "safe" vehicles that barely move and don't keep up with inflation, how will you cover those costs later? Especially when those expenses usually show up at the exact moment your energy, health, and/or cognitive ability are declining?

This is where that false sense of security really hurts. You think you're protected because your principal is intact on paper, but you're actually vulnerable to the one thing that could wipe you out.

LET ME TELL YOU WHAT "SAFE" REALLY MEANS

Most people define safety as "not losing money." But that's only half the equation.

True safety is the ability to meet your needs, now and in the future, without fear, without guesswork, and without sacrificing your lifestyle. That requires more than a pile of stable assets. It requires a plan that is coordinated, not just cautious. The biggest risk isn't a bad market year. It's a bad sequence of expenses when you're unprepared.

> **Ray's Rule #2**
> The biggest risk isn't a bad market year. It's a bad sequence of expenses when you're unprepared.

When I develop a plan designed to align with your goals, here's where we focus:

- Withdrawal Order: Which accounts' funds years 1 to 3, 4 to 14, and 15 and beyond?
- Shock Absorbers: How do we align near-term income strategies with market conditions while allocating long-term assets toward growth consistent with inflation-aware goals?
- Healthcare Buffer: How will you prepare for rising healthcare costs without cannibalizing your lifestyle?
- Longevity Fuel: How will you ensure your income lasts, even if you live to ninety-five or beyond?

These are the kinds of questions you should be asking yourself as you create a coordinated strategy based on your risk capacity, objectives, and personal financial picture.

Speaking of risk capacity, let's talk about how that is much different than risk tolerance.

RISK TOLERANCE VS. RISK CAPACITY: THE DIFFERENCE THAT MATTERS

Most folks I meet have built a portfolio that aligns with their risk tolerance or how much market volatility they can emotionally stomach. While that's important, it shouldn't be the only driver. The other driver, especially in retirement, is your *risk capacity*. This is how much risk your plan can afford without jeopardizing designed outcomes.

In plain terms, risk tolerance is what you feel. Risk capacity is what you can afford.

A personal example: my youngest son is seventeen and headed to college soon. We have funds allocated for his college expenses, which will start next year (fingers crossed!). Now, I personally have a high risk tolerance. I can stomach volatility for potentially greater returns. Psychologically, no problem. But these college funds? They *do not* have a high risk capacity. Because we'll need this money within the next year to four years (fingers still crossed!), a market downturn could have a serious impact on the amount of funds available to support his college expenses.

See the difference? Retirement works the same way. If you're drawing income, have a spouse to support, or need to preserve assets for future healthcare or legacy needs, your capacity may be far lower than your tolerance, especially if a market downturn could force you to sell investments at a loss.

Look, I'll be honest with you. I think those risk tolerance questionnaires most advisors use are more in their best interests than in yours! Think about it; if I have cancer and go to the doctor, I wouldn't want a doctor who is going to ask me how I feel about chemo or radiation and build a treatment around my feelings. I would expect a recommended treatment plan based on outcomes, and then a discussion to decide what I'm comfortable with. Your plan for retirement deserves the same respect. A good financial plan doesn't just make you feel comfortable. It is designed to make sure you're financially protected. That's why you should always lead with capacity first and match your investments to the outcomes you need, not just the returns you want.

> **Ray's Rule #3**
> Lead with risk capacity. Let tolerance influence the mix, but never overrule the math.

A BETTER WAY FORWARD: TIME-WEIGHTED ASSET ALLOCATION

If you've been relying on "safe" investments because you're afraid of volatility, you're not wrong to be cautious. Caution is good. But caution without strategy is just fear in a nice suit.

My investment philosophy is time-weighted asset allocation[3]. Here's how it works: we align dollars with the job they need to do and the time they have to do it:

THREE TIME BUCKETS:

1. Now (Years 0 to 3): Stability first. This bucket covers planned withdrawals, known expenses, and "sleep-well" cash for emergencies. Its job is to be there when you need it.

2. Later (Years 4 to 14): Growth with shock absorbers. This money should have moderate growth potential with risk controls, so it can refill the "Now" bucket over time without wild swings.

3. Never (Years 15 and beyond): This is the money designated to create a legacy. We want to outrun inflation and pursue real growth.

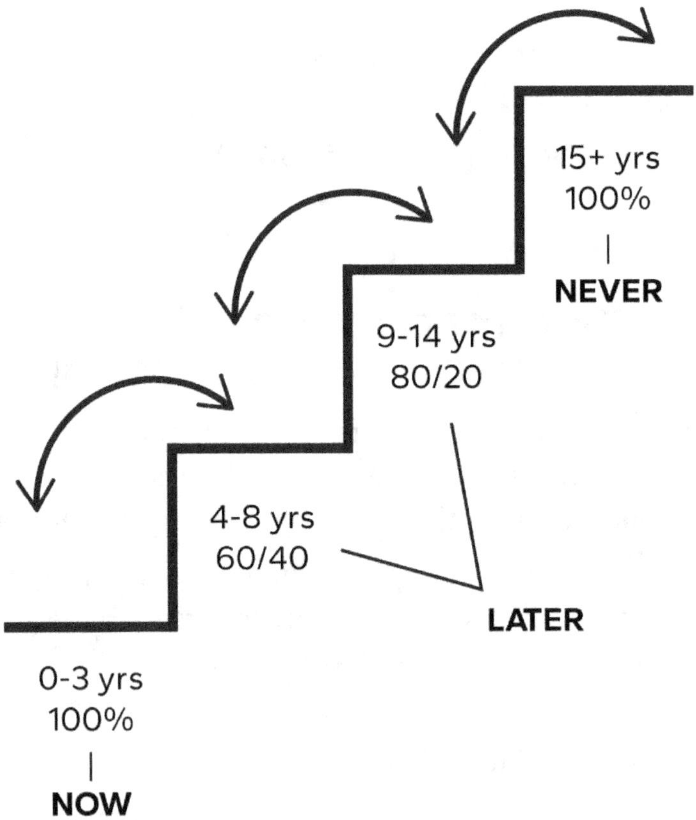

→ Asset Allocation is a method of diversification which positions assets among major investment categories. This investment strategy may be used in an effort to manage risk and enhance returns. However, it does not guarantee a profit or protect against a loss in a declining market.

This usually helps people relax a bit. It makes more sense than when I used to just tell people, "Having all your money in CDs and fixed vehicles may be hurting you." That just made them think, "Oh great, here's another flashy wealth manager trying to push stocks."

Let's give every dollar a job description rather than hiding it all in CDs forever or overexposing our near-term needs to market storms.

This will allow you to use the right mix of tools that are designed to protect, grow, and give you flexibility when things change. Because things *will* change.

Ray's Rule #4
Money without an assignment will default to anxiety. Give every dollar a job.

SEQUENCE OF RETURNS VS. SEQUENCE OF SPENDING

Markets don't hurt retirees merely by going down; they pose a greater challenge when you're forced to withdraw during the down years. That's the sequence of returns problem. But sequence of spending is a twin risk most people ignore. This is when big, lumpy expenses land at the wrong time with no funding strategy. Your plan needs protection for both sequences. Time-weighted asset allocation is designed to provide a near-term spending runway and a long-term growth engine to refuel it.

THE BOTTOM LINE

Let's redefine what safe really means.

Safe is not the absence of risk. Safe is having a coordinated plan that helps protect your future while empowering your present. Safe is sleeping well knowing your money is working just as hard for you now as you worked for it all those years before.

That's the difference between a retiree who worries and one who lives well. "Don't lose money" sounds wise. But in retirement, the smarter mandate is "Don't lose control." We want to maintain control over our income, taxes, healthcare choices, lifestyle, and legacy. Control comes from coordinating our assets, not just being conservative with them.

Successful retirement requires the financial security to sleep well at night and a reason to wake up in the morning. This chapter has been about the financial security part. But as we'll see in the next chapter, having that security doesn't automatically mean you're ready to enjoy your retirement.

YOUR CHAPTER 1 CHECKPOINT

Take a moment to reflect on these questions:

1. Are you more focused on avoiding losses today than ensuring purchasing power for twenty to thirty years?
2. If inflation averages at 3 to 4 percent per year, will your current strategy keep up with rising costs?
3. Do you understand the difference between what you can emotionally handle (risk tolerance) and what your money actually needs to do (risk capacity)?

Mini-Exercise:

List your accounts on a sheet of paper. Label each one **Now (0 to 3)**, **Later (4 to 14)**, or **Never (15 and beyond)**. Is any bucket empty? Does any bucket seem overfilled?

CHAPTER 2

"JUST IN CASE" PARALYSIS: THE PSYCHOLOGY OF UNDER-LIVING

Learn how to spend with confidence, so you enjoy the years that are most spendable without jeopardizing the years that are most vulnerable.

THE COST OF WAITING

MARY[4] SAT ACROSS FROM me with a stack of account statements spread between us. Her husband Bill had passed away six months earlier at age eighty-four. The statements showed over $2 million in their retirement accounts, which is more than they ever imagined.

She looked at the numbers and started crying.

"We were waiting for the right time to enjoy it," she said. "I guess we missed it."

Bill and Mary had retired with $1.8 million. Despite having a strong portfolio, they'd continued to live on just $45,000 per year, which was barely more than their Social Security. They delayed trips. Skipped home upgrades. Declined family vacations. Year after year, they kept saving. Kept worrying. Kept sacrificing.

Just in case.

When Bill died, they still had more money than they'd ever imagined. But what Mary wanted most was one more trip together. One more family vacation. One more memory.

The money couldn't buy that anymore.

Ray's Rule #5
Money can buy freedom, but it cannot buy back time.

The great irony of retirement is that after years of financial discipline, many retirees struggle to flip the switch. The habits that made them successful accumulators now trap them in a cycle of fear, frugality, and unnecessary deprivation. This might be the biggest challenge I've seen in my years of financial planning.

This chapter is about that trap and how to break it. We're going to look at why the accumulation mindset that served you so well for forty years becomes your enemy in retirement, how to recognize when you're suffering from "just in case" paralysis, and what a structured spending plan looks like. This is a plan that gives you permission to enjoy what you've built while still protecting what matters most.

WHAT IT LOOKS LIKE WHEN YOU GET IT RIGHT

So what was happening with Bill and Mary? For decades, they'd been trained to save. "Don't touch your principal." "Prepare for the worst." That mindset worked during their working years, but in retirement, it became a trap. They defaulted to what felt safe by spending as little as possible. This isn't financial prudence. It's financial paralysis.

Mark and Eileen[5] took a different path than Bill and Mary. They were similar ages with similar assets. But they made a different decision because they built a clear spending plan.

When we sat down together, we built that plan. They saw their numbers. We saw what was predictable, what was flexible, and what was protected. Together, we determined what they could pull from their accounts, how it all worked together. And once they could see it laid out clearly, they felt confident. They knew exactly what they could spend, especially during those Go-Go years (roughly the first ten to twelve years of retirement when energy and health typically peak). They began to live intentionally.

They bought a beach condo. Took annual trips with their grandkids. Supported a local charity. And they did this without guilt or anxiety. The difference was clarity because they knew the numbers worked.

So what made the difference between Bill and Mary's story and Mark and Eileen's? Both couples had the money. Both had worked hard. Both had saved diligently.

The difference was a spending plan and the permission that comes with it.

Ray's Rule #6
Clarity creates confidence;
confidence unlocks experiences.

FEAR OF SPENDING

Samantha[6] had over half a million dollars saved. Her essential expenses were completely covered. She was in great financial shape.

Then, during one of the hottest weeks we'd had in years, her air conditioning failed. The repair would take a day or two. A nearby hotel room would cost $180 for the night.

I was surprised when she called me. She wasn't exactly asking permission but clearly looking for reassurance. "Do you think I should just tough it out?" she asked. "I mean, it's only a couple of days."

It was 95 degrees outside and likely even hotter inside her house!

I flat-out said to her, "Samantha, I've never met anybody on their deathbed who regretted spending $180 on being comfortable during a heat wave."

The fact that she even called me looking for reassurance tells you everything about the psychology we're dealing with here. There was a psychological barrier that made reasonable spending seem dangerous. She knew she could afford it. She knew the answer to her own question. But decades of discipline had created such deep-rooted patterns that she needed to hear someone else confirm she was making the right choice.

This is what a dedicated advisor relationship looks like. They are not someone who gives you permission to spend your own money but someone who helps you overcome the psychological barriers that decades of saving have created. It's not just "how did my portfolio perform?" It's "I know the plan says I can afford this, but I need to hear you confirm what I already know so I can move forward with confidence."

That's a whole different level of trust.

Ray's Rule #7

In retirement, the hardest check to write is the one to yourself.

Samantha's story is Bill and Mary's story on a smaller scale. Both faced the same psychological barrier with the inability to give themselves permission to spend money they'd worked hard to save. And if you're reading this thinking, "I would've toughed out the heat, too," then you need to take a deep look at what's really going on.

RECOGNIZING THE PATTERN: HOW DO YOU KNOW IF THIS IS YOU?

If you recognize these patterns, you might be under-living:

Endless second-guessing of withdrawals. You are frequently questioning everything, even though nothing has actually changed in your situation. Most often, I see this during down markets when clients call wanting to cut or pause recurring withdrawals even though the plan says they're okay.

You're obsessed with not touching principal. You'll say things like, "Can we just live off the interest?" as if spending what you saved is some kind of failure rather than the point of retirement savings.

You can't shake the anxiety, even when the numbers say you're fine. This is where the math and the emotions don't line up. On paper, everything works. But you still can't enjoy it.

If you start to notice this behavior, it is a good time to pause, re-read your plan, or call your financial advisor for a "permission recalibration."

Emotional Red Flags:

- Guilt after discretionary purchases
- Fear of "jinxing" good markets by enjoying them
- Relief when your plans get cancelled because "we saved the money"

HOW MARK AND EILEEN BROKE THROUGH

So how did Mark and Eileen get it right when so many others struggle?

A SPENDING PLAN THAT GRANTS PERMISSION

A plan isn't a spreadsheet; it's a story about how your money supports your life. Here's the framework I use with clients. It's the same structure that helped Mark and Eileen move forward with confidence.

STEP 1: COVER YOUR ESSENTIALS WITH PREDICTABLE INCOME

We start with the non-negotiable expenses, like food, housing, medical, utilities, and transportation. We help ensure these expenses are covered by reliable sources of income like Social Security, pensions, and, where appropriate, carefully structured annuity income (tradeoffs are fees, liquidity and surrender charges, and the claims paying ability of the issuer). Your goal is to rest easy, knowing your essential expenses are covered.

STEP 2: MAP OUT YOUR LIFESTYLE SPENDING

Identify the joy purchases, like eating out, traveling, hobbies, family experiences, and things along those lines. Put realistic annual numbers on them, especially during the Go-Go years.

STEP 3: PLAN FOR DISCRETIONARY AND LEGACY GOALS

The next step is layering in discretionary spending, such as charitable giving, gifts to family, and those big bucket-list items. Decide what matters, when it matters, and what would make you proud later.

STEP 4: LOOK THREE YEARS AHEAD (IRREGULAR EXPENSES)

Not all expenses are monthly or even annual. Ask yourself, "What large expenses do I have coming up this year, next year, the year after?"

We look at big trips planned. We look at things like buying a new car, weddings, home renovations, etc.

I like to plan these expenses three years out. Because if you're going to need $75,000 in two years to put an addition on the house, we need to have that money positioned properly right now in a safe place where a market downturn won't derail your plan.

STEP 5: IDENTIFY FUNDING SOURCES

Once you know your expenses, review your accounts, and come up with a plan to identify where you're going to get that money from. It's important to understand where your money is coming from and how you will fund your expenses. This is where coordination and tax strategy come into play without adding unnecessary complexity.

That's what changed everything for Mark and Eileen. Once they could see their numbers clearly in what was predictable, what was flexible, and what was protected, they felt confident in their spending.

YOU'LL ADAPT, BUT YOU CAN'T GET THESE YEARS BACK

Humans are incredibly good at adapting.

Most retirees naturally reduce spending as years pass. Oftentimes, this is not by choice. Our bodies and our health are going to make us adjust before we have to mentally. As we age, we naturally slow down. We travel less. Our hobbies change.

This is where my perspective has changed so much since I started doing this work.

I used to focus only on making sure the money would last. Now I ask a different question. What if you make it to ninety with plenty of money left, but you can't remember the last time you did something that made you feel alive?

I frame it this way: "If you're spending $25,000 a year on travel right now, and in ten years you can only spend $12,000, will you adapt?"

I've never had anyone say no. Of course, you'll adapt. You always do.

But you can't adapt to wasted time. You can't go back and reclaim your sixties. You can't redo the years when your knees still worked, and your grandkids were small, and your spouse was healthy.

That's what Bill and Mary learned too late.

Ray's Rule #8

Front-load joy while you have the health to enjoy it.

THE TAKEAWAY

If you've spent your life saving "just in case," you're not alone. But retirement isn't about stockpiling wealth. It's about living abundantly with confidence. Under-living often masquerades as prudence. The cure isn't reckless spending; it's aligned spending.

So, make that spending plan today because you didn't save all that money just to hoard it. You saved it, so you could use it to create a life worth remembering. Create a plan that protects essentials, funds near-term experiences, and reserves for irregular costs without sacrificing long-term independence. The plan should give you language and limits. It tells you, "Yes, we can book that trip," and "No, let's wait on the second home," with reasons you can trust.

In the next chapter, we're going to talk about how you can coordinate your retirement withdrawals in a way that can influence your taxes over time. It's not about complicated tax loopholes or aggressive strategies. Spending with confidence isn't just about psychology; it's about withdrawal order and taxes. It's about understanding how your IRA and 401(k) actually work, and making simple decisions today that help protect your money tomorrow. This is where thoughtful planning can really pay off . . . literally.

YOUR CHAPTER 2 CHECKPOINT

Take a moment to reflect on these questions:

1. Do you find yourself holding back on travel, hobbies, or experiences because you're afraid of "what if"?
2. Do you know how much you can safely spend each year, or are you guessing?
3. Will you look back one day and regret the trips not taken and memories not made, even though you had the money?

Mini-Exercise:

Draft your Permission Plan. List:

1. Essential Expenses and predictable income sources
2. Lifestyle line items with annual amounts
3. Irregular expenses for the next three years with target dates, and
4. The specific accounts that fund each.

Circle any category without a clearly assigned funding source. That's your next action.

CHAPTER 3

THE TAX TIME BOMB: WHEN THE GOVERNMENT OWNS PART OF YOUR RETIREMENT

Ray's Rule #9

Reclaim what's rightfully yours by making sure the IRS gets only what it's owed, not a penny more.

YOUR SILENT PARTNER

"WE HAVE $1 MILLION saved in our IRA."

"That's great," I often reply. "But how much of it is actually yours?"

Cue the confusion.

Most retirees assume their IRA or 401(k) belongs fully to them, or their spouse, or their children when they pass. But if your savings are tax-deferred, you have a silent partner. And that partner is the IRS.

Unlike you, they don't take market risk. They just wait. They wait for the account balance to grow. They wait until you start withdrawing. They wait until your spouse becomes a widow(er). They wait until your children inherit.

That's when the tax bill comes due.

In this chapter, we'll discuss why tax-deferred accounts can create unintended tax challenges over time, the widow's tax trap that catches most couples completely off guard, how to take back control before it's too late, and how the SECURE Act changed everything about what you're really leaving to your kids.

YOUR IRA ISN'T REALLY YOURS

Let me explain what I mean by "silent partner."

When I meet with people, I start asking questions. Is this a traditional 401(k) or IRA? Do you know what that means? Have you heard of Required Minimum Distributions (RMDs)? Do you know why the IRS makes you take them? Do you know the difference between tax-deferred and tax-free?

Then I explain that this money went in tax-deferred, not tax-free. There's a huge difference between those two words.

Traditional IRAs are commonly described as tax-deferred accounts, where taxes on contributions and earnings are generally deferred until funds are withdrawn.

Roth IRAs are often described as tax-advantaged or tax-free accounts because qualified withdrawals may be received free of federal income tax under current law, provided applicable requirements are met.

When these Traditional IRA's were created decades ago, no one fully explained the tradeoff. Everyone thought, "This is fantastic. I'm reducing my income. I'm not paying taxes on it." It felt like free money. But you didn't avoid taxes. You postponed them.

You didn't pay tax when you contributed the money, so the IRS is waiting to take its cut when you withdraw it. That might be 10 percent, 12 percent, 22 percent, or even 37 percent, depending on your income bracket and how you handle your withdrawals.

The problem with this is that most retirees don't have a withdrawal strategy. Instead, they simply take out what they need or wait until the IRS forces them to take RMDs; that's not a plan. If your retirement plan doesn't factor in how, when, where, and *who* will pay those taxes, it's not a real plan.

THE WIDOW'S TAX BRACKET SQUEEZE

Richard and Helen[7] had been retired for five years when Richard passed away suddenly at seventy-six. On paper, they had done everything right. They filed jointly, paid 12 percent taxes on most of their retirement income, maximized both Social Security checks, and took their RMDs from Richard's old 401(k).

Their combined income was made up of Richard's Social Security of $2,800 monthly, Helen's Social Security of $1,900 monthly, plus approximately $30,000 annually in RMDs from their retirement accounts. Their total income was around $86,400 per year. Filing jointly, they were comfortably in the 12 percent tax bracket.

Then Richard died.

Helen kept the larger Social Security check, which was Richard's at $2,800. But Helen's $1,900 check stopped. Gone. Just like that, she lost nearly $23,000 in annual income.

The cruel part is that the RMDs didn't stop. The bills didn't stop. Helen still needed roughly the same amount of money to live on. Now she's filing as a single taxpayer with similar income needs.

Suddenly, Helen's effective tax rate jumped. Single filer brackets income levels are lower than married filing jointly. That income that used to be taxed at 12 percent? Now portions of it were being taxed at 22 percent.

This is what is referred to as the widow's tax trap: same expenses, smaller income, potential higher tax rates.

But there's hope because you can plan for this. Thoughtful withdrawal sequencing, selective Roth conversions, and coordinated income sources may cushion your surviving spouse long before the IRS gets its share.

Ray's Rule #10

The time to protect your spouse from the widow's tax trap is while you're both still here.

THREE WAYS TO TAKE BACK CONTROL

You have more influence over your tax future than most people realize. Here are three primary ways to approach future tax planning decisions.

ROTH CONVERSIONS: PAY NOW, SAVE LATER

While Roth conversions are not appropriate for everyone, they may provide greater flexibility and potential tax advantage in the future. Roth conversions turn tax-deferred assets into tax-free ones under the current tax laws. Qualified Roth withdrawals (after meeting holding periods and age requirements) are generally income tax free. Here's how I explain Roth conversions to clients. We're going to gradually, year by year, move some money from your traditional IRA into a Roth IRA. Yes, you'll pay taxes on that conversion. But here's what you get in return:

- **Tax-free income.** Once assets are in a Roth and withdrawals are qualified, they can be distributed income-tax-free for you, your spouse, and potentially your heirs.
- **Lower RMDs down the road.** Less money in traditional IRAs means smaller required distributions later.
- **Protection for your surviving spouse.** They'll have tax-free money to draw from, helping manage income and reduce the risk of higher tax brackets.
- **A real inheritance for your kids.** Roth IRAs generally are tax-free assets though required distribution rules may still apply.

I call this bracket-filling. Every year, you should look at your projected tax return and figure out how much can be converted while staying in your current bracket without pushing you into the next one. It's strategic, not random.

One critical thing: You should never do a Roth conversion without talking to your tax professional.

RMD PLANNING: MORE THAN THE MINIMUM

It's called a required *minimum* distribution. That's the smallest amount you should be taking out. It doesn't mean you can't take out more.

Don't wait until the government requires you to take RMDs to start thinking about withdrawals. You should look at how distributions will affect your tax brackets, Income-Related Monthly Adjustment Amount (IRMAA) surcharges, which are basically higher Medicare premiums for higher income levels, and Social Security taxation years in advance.

If you retire at sixty-five and you're not working anymore, you might be in a really low tax bracket. Maybe you're living off Social Security and some savings, and you're only in the 12 percent bracket. That's the perfect time to start pulling money out of your IRAs, even before you're required to. Pay the tax while you're in the low bracket instead of waiting until you're seventy-three when RMDs kick in and push you into the 22 percent or 24 percent bracket.

I tell clients all the time that we're always exploring the impact of taking out additional money. It's not just what you're required to take but what makes sense for your long-term tax picture[8].

Ray's Rule #11

If you wait until the IRS tells you what to withdraw or let them determine the amount you need to withdraw, you're not in control - the government is.

QUALIFIED CHARITABLE DISTRIBUTIONS: GIVE SMART

If you're charitably inclined, this strategy is powerful. Once you're age 70½, you can send money directly from your IRA to a qualified charity. That money doesn't count as income, so you don't pay tax on it. It's one of the most tax-efficient ways to give.

Having your distribution allocated as a Qualified Charitable Distribution (QCD) could be more beneficial than having the money given to you and then writing a check to the charity.

But there's a catch. You must tell your tax preparer. Your 1099 will show the full withdrawal without indicating the charitable gift. I've seen people pay taxes on money they gave away because their CPA didn't know where it went. Keep the charity's receipt, and make sure your tax preparer knows before filing.

THE SECURE ACT: THE END OF THE STRETCH IRA

Before 2020, when your children inherited your IRA, they could stretch those withdrawals over their entire lifetime. Not anymore.

The SECURE Act changed all that. Now in most instances, when a non-spouse inherits your IRA, they have to empty the entire account within ten years, often during their peak earning years when they're already in their highest tax bracket.

If you leave your $800,000 IRA to your daughter and she's in the 32 percent tax bracket, she could easily lose $250,000 or more to taxes.

Inheritance feels like "found money" to the kids. They don't realize they need a strategy to take it out over that ten-year window in the most tax-efficient way. So they take it all at once as a lump sum, which pushes them into even higher tax brackets.

It absolutely breaks my heart when I see 30 percent to 40 percent of Mom and Dad's hard-earned money go straight to Uncle Sam because nobody planned for this.

> **Ray's Rule #12**
>
> You can't control the laws that Congress passes, but you can control how prepared your family is.

THE BOTTOM LINE

You didn't work for decades to hand over a third of your savings to the IRS at the finish line.

You have more influence over your taxes than you've been told if you plan frequently and in a timely manner.

Tax planning in retirement isn't about beating the system. It's about maximizing the life your money can support, and minimizing what leaks out through inaction.

The good news is, these are fixable problems with planning. But only if you stop treating your IRA as "your money" and start seeing it as an account subject to future tax obligations. Every year you delay action, your obligations may grow. By planning early with deliberate strategies like evaluating conversions, strategic distributions/withdrawals, and smart giving, you can regain influence over how, when, and to what extent your retirement savings are taxed and take ownership of your retirement story.

In the next chapter, we're going to talk about scattered accounts across multiple institutions, which is another problem I see a lot. You might think having accounts at different banks and investment companies means you're diversified. But there's a big difference between diversification and just having your money in different places. When your accounts aren't coordinated, you're missing opportunities, and that may cost you money.

YOUR CHAPTER 3 CHECKPOINT

Take a moment to reflect on these questions:

1. Have you thought about how much of your IRA or 401(k) really belongs to you, and how much belongs to the IRS?
2. Have you discussed Roth conversions or bracket-filling strategies with your financial advisor and tax professional?
3. Have you considered how Required Minimum Distributions (RMDs) will impact your taxes later and your surviving spouse's taxes?
4. Do you have a plan for managing withdrawals in a tax-efficient way, or will you just take what you need when you need it?

Mini-Exercise:

Print your latest retirement account statements. Write "IRS" next to 20 to 30 percent of the balance. That's roughly your tax obligation. Now decide how much of that you'd rather keep and start planning to make that happen.

CHAPTER 4

SCATTERED SUCCESS: WHEN MULTIPLE ACCOUNTS CREATE MULTIPLE PROBLEMS

I'LL NEVER FORGET THE day Tina[9] walked into my office. She had a tote bag full of statements. When we started looking into them, she had accounts at eight different banks spread across three towns.

Every time she walked into a bank, someone would convince her to open a new account with some small perk. Maybe a slightly better rate here and a bonus there. At first, it didn't seem like a big deal. But after a while, it turned into a headache. She had statements coming from all directions, minimum balances to keep track of, and money scattered in places she sometimes forgot about. It was then that I asked, "If something happened to you tomorrow, how would your children find it all?" Silence. This is the burden none of us wants to leave behind. For her kids to help settle her affairs, they would've had to chase down every account, figure out what was where, and hope nothing slipped through the cracks.

It's the same with investment accounts. Having multiple accounts doesn't automatically mean you're safer or better diversified. Sometimes it just means more confusion, more fees, tax mistakes, and more potential for errors. And none of these accounts are coordinated toward your goals.

In this chapter, we'll discuss why having accounts at different institutions doesn't mean you're diversified, what happens when your financial team doesn't communicate, the difference between consolidation and coordination, and why getting this right matters for you now and for your family after you're gone.

DIFFERENT IS NOT DIVERSIFIED

A lot of people think that because they have accounts at different banks or investment companies, they're diversified. But diversification isn't the number of accounts you hold. More importantly, it's what is *inside* those accounts.

For example, you might have a 401(k) from an old job, an IRA at a brokerage firm, and a taxable investment account somewhere else. On paper, that might seem spread out and diversified. But if all of those accounts are invested in similar large-cap U.S. stock funds, then you're not really diversified at all. You're just holding the same type of investment in three different places.

True diversification[10] means having a mix of assets that balances roles and risks across:

- **Asset classes:** stocks, bonds, real assets, risk-managed tools.
- **Time horizons:** near-term income vs. long-term growth.
- **Tax treatments:** taxable, tax-deferred, potentially tax-free or tax-advantaged (potentially tax-free).

Without that, multiple accounts can cause a false sense of security while hiding overlaps and gaps.

The goal isn't more accounts, it's more coordination. You want to pull everything into one clear strategy, so you can see where you're truly diversified, where you're exposed, and how to make your money work together efficiently.

WHEN YOUR PROFESSIONALS DON'T TALK TO EACH OTHER

Typically, different accounts are also attached to different professionals. But when your financial advisor, lawyer, and tax professional aren't on the same page, things fall through the cracks. And usually, you're the one who could pay the price.

You could update your will with an attorney, but the beneficiaries on your retirement accounts were never updated to reflect your desired changes. The attorney assumed the financial advisor would handle it, the financial advisor wasn't aware of the update, and the end result is money may go to the wrong person.

Or consider the difference between working with a tax preparer versus a tax planner. There is a big difference between tax preparation (reporting the past) and tax planning (shaping the future). Your tax professional might file a perfect tax return every April, but if they're not coordinating with your financial advisor about potential Roth conversions, withdrawal strategies, or how your investment decisions affect your taxes, you may be missing opportunities to save thousands of dollars over your retirement.

Later, we will talk about the tax consequences of getting beneficiaries wrong. But this is a different problem. When your professionals don't coordinate, even perfect planning documents can fail.

And then there's the stress factor. You're stuck being the go-between, trying to relay messages between professionals who should be working together in the first place. You can easily get confused and frustrated trying to be the translator between your financial advisor and your tax professional. When everyone's on the same page, your plan works smoothly, and you will help mitigate expensive mistakes or surprises.

So how do we fix this? It starts with understanding an important distinction that most people miss.

CONSOLIDATION VS. COORDINATION: WHAT'S THE DIFFERENCE?

Consolidation and coordination are not the same thing.

Consolidation is when you move all of your accounts to one place with one bank, one brokerage, and one investment firm. That can make things simpler, but it doesn't necessarily make your plan better. You can have all your money under one roof and still have duplication, hidden risks, or a poor tax strategy.

Coordination is making sure every account you have, no matter where it's held, is working together toward your goals. For example, your IRA might be invested one way, your taxable brokerage account another way, and if an annuity is part of your financial plan, it is serving a different purpose. When they're coordinated, you know which dollars to spend first, how to minimize taxes, and how to protect your income over time.

I once worked with a client who had accounts at three different firms. We didn't force transfers. Instead, we assigned jobs and synchronized the accounts. We kept her CD at the local bank, managed her IRA, and left her old 401(k) where it was, but we built a coordinated plan around all of them. She told me later that it was the first time she felt like all her money was finally pulling in the same direction.

Ray's Rule #13
Simplicity is good; synchronization is better.

ADVICE VS. COMPREHENSIVE PLANNING

Advice solves one problem at a time. You ask, "Should I invest in this fund?" or, "Should I take Social Security now?" You get answers. Maybe good answers. But those answers are focused on that single question, never on how it affects everything else.

Comprehensive planning looks at the big picture. Income, investments, tax strategies, estate planning strategies, insurance, and legacy. It shows how the pieces fit together and whether they're aligned with your long-term goals.

Advice creates choices. A plan gives you confidence because the choices work together. That's the difference between having answers and having a plan.

WHAT COORDINATION LOOKS LIKE

Let me show you what I mean by coordination. Here are the four essential planning areas and what happens when they work in isolation versus when they're synchronized:

THE FOUR PIECES OF A COORDINATED RETIREMENT PLAN

Planning Area	When It's Isolated	When It's Coordinated
Tax Planning Strategies	Surprise tax bills, higher brackets, and more of Social Security taxed	Lower lifetime taxes, smoother withdrawals, strategic Roth strategies
Investment Planning	Overlapping/ duplicate strategies and hidden risks	True diversification[11], growth aligned with income needs and timing
Estate Planning Strategies	Beneficiaries misaligned, probate issues, and family conflict	Clear transfers, minimized costs, family protected
Income Planning	Withdrawals from the wrong accounts, income gaps, and spending anxiety	Reliable paychecks, tax-smart withdrawals, confidence to spend

This is why I tell clients: having multiple professionals isn't the problem. Having professionals who don't talk to each other is. When these four pieces operate independently, you get gaps, conflicts, and anxiety. When they're coordinated, you get clarity and confidence.

THE BURDEN YOU'RE LEAVING YOUR FAMILY

Scattered accounts don't just confuse you. They burden your family down the road. It can become a scavenger hunt for your family.

I've seen family members spend months chasing down old statements, calling multiple banks, not knowing what was missing or if accounts were even still open. Sometimes money gets lost because no one knows it exists.

A coordinated plan does more than protect your finances. It gives your family clarity instead of chaos and a legacy that reflects what you worked to build.

HOW TO GET ORGANIZED

When a client comes into my office, the first thing we do is take everything that feels scattered and overwhelming and put it into one clear picture. Most clients have never seen all their accounts, including bank, investment, retirement, and insurance, lined up together with a purpose attached to each one.

Here's how we organize:

- **Income Accounts (NOW: Years 0 to 3)** – Low-volatility sources for scheduled withdrawals and emergencies
- **Growth Accounts (LATER: Years 4 to 14)** – Moderate risk, risk-managed growth to refill the NOW bucket on a cadence
- **Legacy Accounts (NEVER: Years 15 and beyond)** – Money you plan to leave to others, meant for the next generation

Once you have determined the Now/Later/Never classifications, we then put them into a helpful chart. This chart[12] can help with future planning by having a snapshot of where all the money is and the total in each category.

Assets	Now/ Income	Later/ Accumulation	Legacy/ Never	Total
Checking Account	$3,600	-	-	$3,600
Savings Account	$74,900	-	-	$74,900
Employee Stock	-	$115,542	-	$115,542
Health Savings Account	-	$23,210	-	$23,210
Traditional IRA	-	$51,317	-	$51,317
Employer Provided 401(K)	-	$1,250,000	$719,770	$1,969,770
Primary Residence	-	-	$630,000	$630,000
Total Assets	$78,500	$1,440,069	$1,349,770	$2,868,339

When you look at it that way, every account has a job. Instead of eight different buckets you're trying to juggle, you now see a coordinated plan where each piece plays a role.

In Chapter 1, I talked about my time-weighted asset allocation philosophy. That same approach applies here. Once we can see all your accounts in one place, we organize them by when you'll need the money, not by which institution holds it.

This coordination brings the clarity and confidence that comes from knowing each dollar has a role in your bigger plan.

THREE QUESTIONS TO MAKE SURE YOUR TEAM IS WORKING TOGETHER

If you want to know whether your team is truly coordinating, ask three questions:

"When was the last time you spoke with my other advisors?" If they aren't talking, something's falling through the cracks.

"Who's coordinating my tax, investment, and estate strategies?" Most people assume it's happening automatically, but often no one's taking the lead, or you need to take the lead!

"How do you make sure my plan works together, not just in pieces?" Each professional may excel at their specialty, but without someone seeing the big picture, you don't get a real plan.

If you don't get clear answers, that could indicate a gap in coordination.

Ray's Rule #14
Your plan is only as strong as its weakest link.

THE BOTTOM LINE

It's not about having fewer accounts or consolidating everything in one place but having a unified plan. It's about making sure every dollar you've worked so hard to save is working efficiently and in line with your goals. Coordination helps to reduce overlap, prevent mistakes, and frees you to live the life you intended without leaving your family a puzzle to solve.

In the next chapter, we're going to talk about Social Security, which is one of your biggest retirement assets that most people completely mishandle. I'll show you why that filing decision matters more than you realize, and how one mistake can cost you hundreds of thousands of dollars over your lifetime.

YOUR CHAPTER 4 CHECKPOINT

Take a moment to reflect on these questions:

1. Are you juggling accounts instead of having one clear plan of how your money works together?
2. When you make a change in one area, like investments or estate documents, do you know how it affects the others?
3. If something happened to you tomorrow, would your family know where all your accounts are and who to call?

Mini-Exercise:

Draw a triangle and label each side Financial **Advisor**, **Tax Professional**, and **Attorney**. In the center, write **You**. Now draw arrows: which direction does communication flow? One-way? Sporadic? Or coordinated among all four parties?

If any side is blank, that's where coordination and confidence can be strengthened.

CHAPTER 5

THE SOCIAL SECURITY FILING DISASTER: LEAVING MONEY ON THE TABLE FOR LIFE

I'LL NEVER FORGET THE first time I met Linda[13] who had filed for Social Security at sixty-two. She came to see me a few months after starting her benefits, and I could tell something was bothering her.

"I just wanted to get something back after paying in for so many years," she told me. "My friends all said to take it as soon as I could."

When I ran the numbers, my heart sank.

Linda was receiving approximately $1,650 per month. If she had waited until her Full Retirement Age (FRA), she would have received $2,360 per month. Over a twenty-five year retirement, that early filing decision would cost her well over $200,000 in lifetime income.

At the time, it felt like a small decision, but the decision was permanent. So many people treat Social Security like a simple government form. But it's not. It's one of the biggest financial decisions you'll ever make.

In this chapter, we'll discuss why Social Security is one of your largest assets, the three filing mistakes that could cost you money, how couples should coordinate their decisions to protect the surviving spouse, and how to integrate this decision with taxes and overall income planning.

Ray's Rule #15
Social Security is not a form that you file but a foundation that you optimize.

WHY SOCIAL SECURITY IS BIGGER THAN YOU THINK

Social Security is one of the biggest assets you own, even though it doesn't show up on any account statement. If you add up the income it pays over your lifetime, it can easily be worth hundreds of thousands of dollars.

Social Security is special because it's designed to create income for the rest of your life, and it's inflation-adjusted. Two features that private investments struggle to match consistently. No matter what the market does, that check keeps coming every month. And it grows over time to help keep up with rising costs.

When I explain this to clients, they're often skeptical. They'll say, "But what if Social Security runs out?" And I remind them that this is backed by the taxing authority of the federal government. That's different from any private investment vehicle.

Social Security is the foundation of your retirement income plan. Everything else, including IRAs, investments, and annuities, is built on top of it. Treat it with the weight it deserves.

Yet I've watched people spend more time researching which cell phone plan to select than deciding when to file for Social Security. Think about that for a moment. You'll research data plans and coverage maps for hours but treat a decision that will shape the rest of your financial life like a Tuesday afternoon errand.

THREE FILING MISTAKES TO AVOID

In my experience, I've seen the same three mistakes repeatedly, and they may cost people serious money:

1. FILING TOO EARLY WITHOUT UNDERSTANDING THE PERMANENT REDUCTION

When you file at sixty-two, you're reducing your benefit by roughly 25 to 30 percent as compared to your FRA, and that reduction is permanent. For someone entitled to $2,000 at full retirement age, filing at sixty-two means accepting around $1,400 instead. Stretch that out over twenty or thirty years, and you could be leaving $100,000 to $200,000 on the table.

2. NOT COORDINATING AS A COUPLE

For most couples, one Social Security check disappears when one spouse passes. The survivor keeps the higher benefit.

Regardless of which spouse passes away first, the surviving spouse keeps only the higher of the two benefits. That's why it's critical for the higher-earning spouse to consider delaying, as their benefit becomes the survivor benefit.

3. IGNORING HOW SOCIAL SECURITY INTERACTS WITH YOUR OTHER INCOME

Up to 85 percent of your benefits can be taxable depending on how much other income you have. The timing of IRA withdrawals, pensions, and capital gains from investments can raise how much of your Social Security is exposed to tax. Filing at the wrong time or without a plan can increase taxes and reduce net income. With strategic planning, we want to minimize the amount of social security that will be taxable, whenever possible.

Ray's Rule #16

The right filing age depends on your income mix, not your neighbor's birthday.

WHAT THIS LOOKS LIKE WITH A REAL COUPLE

Let me tell you about David and Patricia[14].

David had a much higher benefit at about $3,200 at his full retirement age, compared to Patricia's $1,800. He came into my office ready to file at sixty-two.

"It's my money," he said. "I want it back."

When we ran the numbers, we discovered that if David filed at sixty-two, he'd receive about $2,240 per month. If he waited until seventy, he'd receive almost $4,000 per month.

"David," I said, "you're not just making this decision for yourself. You're making it for Patricia's future security."

David had some health concerns. Patricia came from a family where women routinely lived into their nineties. If David passed away at seventy-five, Patricia would spend potentially twenty more years living on whichever benefit was higher.

If David filed at sixty-two, Patricia's survivor-based benefit would be locked in; the only adjustment she would receive would be the annual cost-of-living adjustment. If he waited until seventy, she'd receive nearly $4,000. Over twenty years, that's a difference of over $400,000 for the person he loved.

David's whole demeanor changed when he saw those numbers.

You need to consider survivor benefits thoughtfully. You're not just making a filing decision. You're making sure the person you love most is taken care of long after you're gone.

Ray's Rule #17

When you file, you're choosing your spouse's survivor check as much as your own.

TAXES AND SOCIAL SECURITY

You can't look at Social Security by itself. It has to connect with your tax planning and the rest of your retirement income strategy. In many cases, delaying Social Security while taking modest IRA withdrawals during lower tax-bracket years, or before withdrawals are required (RMDs), can:

- Fill lower tax brackets now
- Shrink future RMDs
- Reduce the taxation of social security later
- Improve widow/widower outcomes

Social Security, taxes, and retirement income are three parts of the same puzzle. If you don't look at them together, you miss opportunities. This is the coordination we continue to discuss in this book.

FIVE FACTORS TO CONSIDER

When clients come to me ready to file, we sit down with their tax returns, Social Security, investments, and other assets to look at five key factors:

- **Longevity Outlook:** Life expectancy based on family history and health

- **Survivor Impact:** Which filing path best protects the survivor's lifetime income?

- **Other Income Sources**: IRAs, pensions, part-time work, annuities

- **Tax Interactions:** Tax implications of when you claim, current and future brackets, and IRMAA

- **Break-Even Age**: Where delaying overtakes filing early. It's useful but never decisive by itself. Oddly enough, this tends to be the factor most people look at in a vacuum

Each of these factors matters, but none of them matters in isolation. We need to see how they all work together with your complete retirement picture.

UNDERSTANDING THE BREAK-EVEN POINT

A lot of people ask me about the break-even point, which is the age where waiting to file starts to pay off compared to filing early. For most people, it's somewhere around age eighty to eighty-two.

However, filing at sixty-two is like taking a smaller slice of the pie right now. Waiting is like letting the pie keep baking. The pie rises, and once you cut it, you keep eating that bigger slice every month for the rest of your life.

However, if you're facing starvation, you're going to need to eat that small slice of pie right now.

That's the reality. There's no one-size-fits-all answer. You should be considering the trade-offs clearly, so you can make the choice that fits your life, not just the math.

THE BOTTOM LINE

For most retirees, Social Security is the only source of income that's designed to last for life and adjusted for inflation. That steady check every month is what everything else is built on.

This is one of the biggest financial decisions you'll ever make, so treat it that way. Don't wing it.

In the next chapter, we're going to talk about what happens when only one spouse understands the retirement plan. Because even if you make the perfect Social Security decision, if your spouse doesn't know what's going on, you're setting them up for a crisis down the road.

YOUR CHAPTER 5 CHECKPOINT

Take a moment to reflect on these questions:

1. Do you have a written strategy for when to file for Social Security that's based on actual analysis, or are you planning to just "start when you feel ready"?
2. Have you and your spouse talked about how your filing decisions affect each other's lifetime benefits, especially the survivor benefit?
3. Have you coordinated your filing age with IRA withdrawals to reduce lifetime taxes?

Mini-Exercise:

Write down your estimated Social Security benefit at sixty-two, Full Retirement Age, and seventy. Then ask yourself two questions:

1. How long could I live, and what would my lifetime income total look like at each age?
2. If I live longer than expected, which filing age makes me feel most secure that I won't outlive my savings?

For couples: repeat the same exercise using both spouses' benefits and highlight which option maximizes total household income over both of your lifetimes.

CHAPTER 6

THE SILENT PARTNERSHIP: WHEN ONLY ONE SPOUSE KNOWS THE PLAN

"I DON'T EVEN KNOW where to start."

Barbara[15] came into my office three months after her husband, Tom, passed away. She'd been referred by a friend, and when she sat down across from me, she had stacks of account statements. Some she'd found in drawers, others that had arrived in the mail after he died. Every day, it felt like there was a new account being discovered.

Tom had handled everything for their entire marriage. Barbara trusted him completely, and he'd done a good job. But now he was gone, and Barbara was drowning.

She didn't know which accounts were which. She couldn't access anything online because she didn't have the passwords. She had no idea what their monthly expenses actually were because Tom had always paid the bills. When I asked about their investment strategy, she just shook her head.

The irony of this situation is that Barbara had plenty of money. More than enough to maintain her lifestyle comfortably. But she didn't know that, and she was worried about how she was going to make it all work. This is what happens when only one spouse knows the plan. And I see it more often than you'd think.

In this chapter, we'll discuss why both spouses need to understand your retirement strategy, the three biggest risks when only one partner holds the map, how to engage the less-involved spouse without overwhelming them, and when it makes sense to include your adult children in these conversations.

Ray's Rule #18

A good plan fails if only one person knows it.

THE PROBLEM NOBODY SEES COMING

I've learned that everything works fine while both spouses are healthy and the financially-savvy partner is managing things. The crisis hits when something happens, like an illness, cognitive decline, or death. Suddenly, the uninvolved spouse faces overwhelming responsibility at the absolute worst time.

The spouse who's been left out of financial conversations doesn't feel comfortable making decisions because they've never been part of them.

THE THREE FAILURE PATTERNS

When it comes to these scenarios, I see three problems emerge consistently:

PROBLEM #1: PANIC LEADS TO BAD DECISIONS

I once had a widower tell me, "I wish I had paid more attention when my wife was alive. I feel like I'm trying to put together a puzzle without the picture on the box."

His wife had always managed their finances. When she passed, he didn't understand their withdrawal strategy or why money was positioned in different accounts. In his panic and confusion, he made hasty decisions that created unnecessary taxes and added risk he didn't need, all because he didn't know they already had a plan in place.

PROBLEM #2: BECOMING AN EASY TARGET

When you're grieving and overwhelmed, you become vulnerable. I've seen uninvolved spouses say yes to the first person who offers to "help," even when that help comes with high-commission products, unnecessary fees, or strategies that don't fit their situation.

The fact is, when someone doesn't feel confident about finances, they often lean on whoever offers assistance first. That can lead to expensive mistakes.

In general, people should wait at least three months before making long-term decisions with assets left from a loved one. This is the time to grieve and heal. If you rush, you take the risk of making decisions in the wrong state of mind that you might regret later.

PROBLEM #3: MISSING THE BIG PICTURE

Even well-meaning surviving spouses make costly mistakes simply because they don't see how the puzzle pieces fit.

They don't know which accounts to draw from first for tax efficiency. They don't know how their withdrawals might affect Medicare premiums. They don't know when taking a distribution could trigger higher taxes on Social Security. They don't know what strategies could protect more money for their beneficiaries.

Without understanding these connections, smart people make preventable mistakes.

At the end of the day, the plan only works if both people understand it.

HOW TO GET BOTH SPOUSES INVOLVED

The good news? This is fixable. You just need to start the conversation now.

BOTH SPOUSES COME TO PLANNING MEETINGS

I require both spouses at any meeting where we're discussing the plan.

Early on, I'll explain, "I know one of you may take the lead on finances, but these decisions affect both of you. I want to make sure you're both comfortable, because if something happens to either one of you, the other needs to feel confident moving forward. One of you may lead the details, but both of you will live with the outcomes."

You should have the same thinking.

HAVING THE RIGHT-SIZED INVOLVEMENT FOR THE LESS-INVOLVED SPOUSE

I worked with a couple, Robert and Anne[16], where Anne handled everything, and Robert wanted nothing to do with it. He'd say, "That's her job."

I explained, "Robert, if something happens to Anne, these decisions directly affect your income for the rest of your life. This isn't about becoming a financial expert but protecting yourself and your family."

That changed his perspective. Over time, he focused on the decisions that materially impacted his family, income, and security.

MAKING IT EASY TO UNDERSTAND

Some spouses avoid getting involved because understanding finances is not their strong suit. I want to make this as easy for them as I can. I avoid jargon and use plain explanations. Instead of saying "we're rebalancing your asset allocation," I'll say "we're making sure you're not putting all your eggs in one basket."

You should have a simple one-page overview before getting into a detailed analysis. Both spouses can understand what you have, what it's for, who to call.

Consider each spouse's perspective, even if one spouse doesn't know the numbers, they know what matters to them in security, leaving a legacy, and enjoying life today. Ask yourself, "What's most important to me if something happened tomorrow?" Each spouse should feel their voice matters in the plan.

Sometimes I'll suggest updating beneficiaries together as homework. It's simple, involves both people, and builds confidence without being overwhelming. Those small wins build comfort over time.

FOUR THINGS BOTH SPOUSES NEED TO KNOW

You don't need to turn your spouse into a financial expert. But here are four things you both should know:

1. **Where the accounts are and who to call.** Both should know what accounts exist, where they're held, how to access them, and who to contact if something happens;
2. **What income is predictable.** Social Security, pensions, and annuities form your foundation. Know how much income is predictable and what will change when one spouse passes away;
3. **Which accounts serve which purpose.** Income accounts (next few years), growth accounts (five to twenty years out), and legacy accounts (never touching, meant for the next generation);
4. **The tax strategy basics.** You don't need to know tax tables, but understand how withdrawals may affect taxes, especially RMDs and the "widow's tax" from Chapter 3.

You should have a simple one-page summary covering these essentials with the important phone numbers at the top. This will serve as the safety net for the spouse who isn't comfortable with details.

BEING PREPARED

Let me contrast Barbara's story with a different couple I worked with, Michael and Diane[17].

Diane wasn't interested in the financial details, but she always came to our meetings. She'd ask questions, even the "simple" ones, and stayed engaged just enough to understand the plan.

When Michael passed away, Diane called me that week.

"I can't imagine doing this alone," she said. "But because we went through it together, I feel prepared."

She knew where everything was. She understood which accounts served which purpose. She knew who her point person was for questions.

Most importantly, she had confidence.

BRINGING YOUR CHILDREN INTO THE CONVERSATION

I get asked all the time, "When should we bring our kids into these conversations?"

My answer is once the conversation shifts from just retirement income to legacy, estate planning strategies, and caregiving. Essentially, when the plan starts to affect them.

If we're talking about powers of attorney, healthcare decisions, or what happens when one spouse passes away, that's the right time to bring in the children. It prevents confusion later and makes sure everyone knows the plan ahead of time.

GETTING THE TIMING RIGHT

It's also smart to include your children if you have multiple accounts scattered in different places. I've seen families spend months trying to track down assets because no one knew where everything was. When the kids are looped in early, they understand what exists, how it's organized, and who to call when the time comes.

As I get to know people over time, I suggest bringing children into the conversation when it makes natural sense. Maybe during a scheduled visit or when everyone's already gathering for a family event. These are difficult conversations to have, and we don't want to add any pressure by asking for schedules to be rearranged, and for the participants not to be relaxed and together.

WHY THIS PROTECTS MORE THAN MONEY

Sometimes the decisions being made make a lot of sense to the parents, but they can be taken the wrong way if the children aren't made aware of why the decision was made. In these scenarios, I strongly believe in having the children present for certain conversations.

The fact is, money conversations in families aren't just about dollars and cents. They're about respect, fairness, and understanding. When parents make decisions, like leaving different amounts to different children based on need, or setting up trusts with specific conditions, those choices usually come from love and careful thought. But without explanation, they can look like favoritism or punishment.

Adult children don't need to be in every financial meeting, and sometimes they shouldn't be. But they *should* be included once the plan affects them directly. It's about clarity, reducing stress, and protecting the family from unnecessary conflict or confusion down the road.

Ray's Rule #19
Clarity now prevents conflict later.

WHAT TO DO NEXT

If you're the spouse who handles everything, ask yourself if your partner could navigate your finances if you can't. If the answer gives you pause, it's time to change that. Create your one-page summary and have your spouse involved.

And if you're the less-involved spouse, staying in the dark doesn't protect you. It makes you vulnerable. Start simple. Attend the next meeting. Ask one question.

Protecting your spouse means making sure everyone knows how to access what you've built, so no one will be taken advantage of in the future.

In the next chapter, we're going to look at what happens when your desire to help your adult children financially ends up threatening your own retirement security. It's a conversation most parents avoid, but it's one we desperately need to have.

YOUR CHAPTER 6 CHECKPOINT

Take a moment to reflect on these questions:

1. If something happened to you tomorrow, would your spouse know what you own, where it is, and who to call?
2. Do both of you feel comfortable explaining how your retirement income is generated?
3. Are you creating peace of mind for both of you, or is one of you still in the dark?

Mini-Exercise:

Set a timer for fifteen minutes. Together, list:

1. Financial Institutions + last four account numbers
2. Where your income will be coming from for the next twelve months
3. The first three people to call

Stop at fifteen minutes. Whatever isn't obvious to both of you today becomes your to-do this week.

CHAPTER 7

TOXIC GENEROSITY: WHEN FAMILY PLANNING BACKFIRES

FRANK AND CHRISTINE[18] WALKED into my office with a problem they didn't even realize they had.

They were sixty-eight, two years into retirement, with $1.4 million saved. But as I started going through their accounts, something didn't add up. Over the past three years, they'd withdrawn nearly $200,000, and it wasn't for trips or home repairs.

It was all going to their forty-two-year-old son, Tyler.

"It was supposed to be short-term," Christine said. "Just until he got back on his feet."

Frank nodded. "We didn't realize how much it was adding up. We just wanted to be there for him."

As a parent myself, I get it. I understand wanting to help your kids. But I've learned that if helping your children jeopardizes your own security, everyone loses. Worse, you might even be doing more harm than good, because you're training them to depend on help that won't exist when you're gone.

In this chapter, we'll discuss the most common ways I see retirees undermine their own retirement through open-ended support to their adult children, how to set boundaries that protect both generations, and why the best gift you can give your children is making sure you never become their financial burden.

THE THREE COMMON MISTAKES

MISTAKE #1: CO-SIGNING LOANS.

The intention is generous. You want to help your family buy a home or start a business. But if they can't keep up with payments, you are liable at a stage when you can't easily recover.

I worked with Ted[19], who co-signed on his son's business loan. When the business failed, Ted was responsible for over $50,000. He told me, "I thought I was helping my son get ahead. Instead, I'm the one paying the price." It didn't just hurt Ted's retirement; it damaged his relationship with his son and created animosity between his son and his other children.

MISTAKE #2: ONGOING SUPPORT WITHOUT BOUNDARIES.

I see parents covering bills, letting kids move back home "temporarily," providing endless financial help. Little by little, it chips away at retirement savings meant to last decades.

Once, I worked with parents who let their daughter move home for what they thought would be "six months." Six months became six years. They covered food, utilities, and even a car payment. By the time she moved out, they'd drained tens of thousands that they couldn't replace. It even strained their marriage as expectations changed.

MISTAKE #3: PULLING FROM RETIREMENT ACCOUNTS TO BAIL THEM OUT.

The problem? Early withdrawals trigger taxes and sometimes penalties, shrinking your account values and future income much faster than you realize. Worse, if the underlying behavior doesn't change, you'll be asked again, now with less capacity to help.

One couple pulled money from their IRA to pay off their daughter's credit card debt of about $15,000. But that debt came from overspending habits she never fixed. Within two years, she ran the balances right back up. Meanwhile, the parents had triggered taxes on the withdrawal and permanently reduced their retirement savings. Their help solved nothing.

Ray's Rule #20

A bailout without behavior change is an invitation to repeat the crisis.

ASK YOURSELF ONE QUESTION

When clients tell me they want to help their children financially, I always bring it back to this:

Can you help without hurting your own long-term security?

Look at your income, expenses, taxes, and how long money needs to last. Once you see what you need, it's easier to figure out what's left to share. Then put structure around it. Not open-ended support but a one-time gift or specific annual amount built into the plan. And then let them know the plan. Communication is key to making this work.

George and Maria[20] wanted to pay off their son's student loans. When we ran the numbers, writing a big check would've hurt their retirement. Instead, we set up a matching system. They matched his payments dollar-for-dollar for a set period. He built habits, and they kept stability. Their son told them it was the first time he'd really accomplished something financially.

Ray's Rule #21

This isn't about being selfish! Give them a ladder to climb—don't carry them over the wall.

HELPING VS. ENABLING (KNOW THE DIFFERENCE)

- **Helping** moves your child forward (a one-time gift, education support, or a defined bridge while they get back on their feet. It has a clear purpose and endpoint);
- **Enabling** removes the incentive to progress (open-ended subsidies that keep the same problem alive). Your support removes their motivation to stand on their own. It drains your plan and their momentum.

I worked with parents who'd been paying their son's bills for years. They thought they were helping him. When we looked closer, their support had kept him from ever learning to manage money. Once we added structure (amount, duration, milestones) around their help, he started taking responsibility. And the parents finally felt relief.

THE SANDWICH GENERATION

Many retirees aren't just dealing with adult children. You're also caring for aging parents while protecting your own retirement.

Alan and Joyce[21] came to me completely overwhelmed. They were paying for Alan's mother's assisted living and covering their daughter's rent. When we mapped it out, it was unsustainable.

We restructured. Alan's mother's care was partly covered by insurance and benefits. They set a clear timeline and budget for their daughter. Joyce later said, "It felt like we were in the middle of everyone's crisis. Setting those boundaries permitted us to help without feeling guilty."

The sandwich generation challenge isn't just money. It's the emotional cost of being pulled in three directions. You're managing parents' healthcare, helping kids get established, and maintaining your own life. A clear financial plan reduces at least one layer of stress.

Ray's Rule #22

A plan can't solve every emotion - but it can remove financial ambiguity so you can lead with love and limits.

HAVING THAT CONVERSATION (WITHOUT FIGHTING)

Once you've made the plan, you need to have the conversation. Start with honest, caring language. "We love you and want to support you, but we have to make sure our retirement stays secure. Here's what we can do, and here's what we can't."

If it helps, you can take the emotion out by saying, "Our financial advisor showed us we can afford this much, but not more."

When you explain your reasoning, most adult children respond well to honest boundaries. Most times, they'll agree it makes sense.

WHEN YOU DON'T WANT TO BECOME A BURDEN

When you set financial boundaries with your children, you're not being selfish. You're being *protective* of them.

The best gift you can give your children isn't more money today. It's the promise that you won't become their financial burden tomorrow.

I've seen people move in with their children, not because of medical needs, but because they gave away so much they couldn't afford their own home anymore. The adult children who once appreciated all that help? Now they're stressed, resentful, and financially strained, trying to support their parents.

That's not the legacy any parent wants.

Think about what happens when you deplete your retirement while helping your kids today. In ten to fifteen years, you'll need help. Your children will be in their peak earning years, raising their own families. They'll be forced to choose between your needs and their own children's futures. The "help" you gave them earlier now costs them far more, not just financially, but emotionally.

When you protect your retirement, you're protecting your children from having to support you later. You're ensuring they can be there for their own children without the weight of another generation on their shoulders. You're modeling that taking care of yourself isn't selfish. It's responsible.

Saying "no" to some requests today isn't selfish. It's one of the most loving things you can do for your family's long-term future.

THE BOTTOM LINE

Supporting family is a wonderful goal, but it has to be done within a plan that protects your security first.

Set clear boundaries. Build a structure around your help. Saying "yes" to your children in a way that protects your retirement is far more loving than saying "yes" to everything and jeopardizing both your futures.

In the next chapter, we're going to talk about what you do with your independence in finding purpose, staying connected, and building a retirement that gives you a reason to get out of bed every morning.

YOUR CHAPTER 7 CHECKPOINT

Take a moment to reflect on these questions:

1. Do you know exactly how much family support your plan can sustain, and for how long, without hurting your own retirement?
2. Are you confident your generosity is *helping* your loved ones become more independent or are you *enabling* them to remain dependent on you?
3. Have you had an honest conversation with your adult children about what you can and can't do financially, or are you avoiding that discussion?

Mini-Exercise:

On a blank sheet of paper, do the following:

1. List every current or requested support item (who/what/how much)
2. Label each as **Helping** or **Enabling** (purpose + endpoint vs open-ended)
3. Set limits (amount, duration, trigger events, review dates)
4. Draft a three-sentence message you can share with your loved one

CHAPTER 8

THE LONELINESS TRAP: WHEN FINANCIAL SECURITY ISN'T ENOUGH

JAMES[22] HAD RECENTLY RETIRED with a solid financial plan in place. I asked him how retirement was going, and he just shook his head.

"Every day feels the same," he told me. "I wake up, have my coffee, and then . . . nothing. I don't know what to do with myself."

For decades, James had led teams, solved problems, and mentored younger employees. Now all of that was gone. Overnight, the meetings stopped, and so did the meaning he got from them.

This is the retirement trap nobody warns you about. You can have all the financial security in the world and still feel completely lost.

Ray's Rule #23
Money funds retirement. Meaning fills it.

In this chapter, we'll discuss why having enough money doesn't guarantee retirement happiness, the four nonfinancial challenges that derail even financially secure retirees, and practical steps you can take right now to build a fulfilling retirement.

WHAT REALLY MAKES RETIREMENT WORK

When clients ask me if they're ready to retire, I look at three things:

1. **Income you can count on.** Predictable sources covering your essential expenses;
2. **Risk awareness and planning.** A plan for taxes, market downturns, and healthcare costs;
3. **Purpose and enjoyment.** Living the retirement you dreamed about, not just living day to day.

FOUR CHALLENGES THAT MONEY CAN'T FIX

Now, I'm not a therapist or a life coach. I'm a financial planner. But I can tell that I've seen these four challenges drive otherwise smart people to make terrible financial decisions.

1. **Loss of identity.** For decades, people defined themselves by their careers. We introduce ourselves by what we do. "I'm an engineer." "I'm a teacher." "I'm a manager." When that disappears, we can struggle with "Who am I now?" One client told me, "I used to introduce myself with my job title. Now, I don't know what to say." He'd spent thirty years defining himself one way, and suddenly that was gone;

2. **Loss of routine.** Work gives structure to your days and weeks. Without it, every day feels the same, and boredom sets in quickly;

3. **Loneliness.** I worked with a widow whose husband had always been the social one. After he passed, she withdrew. Her finances were strong; her circle wasn't;

4. **Misaligned expectations between spouses.** I worked with William and Betty[23] who retired at the same time. Betty wanted airports and adventures. William wanted home and hobbies. They'd planned their finances, not their weeks. They hadn't talked about what came next, and their retirement started with frustration instead of fulfillment.

My experience has shown me that the human spirit can adapt more easily to financial changes than emotional ones.

WHAT WORRIES ME MOST

When someone feels isolated or lacks purpose, they often look for ways to fill the void. And that's when I see the financial damage start to happen.

I worked with a widow, Grace[24], who started giving large sums to family and charities almost immediately after her husband passed. When we sat down together, she admitted, "I was just trying to feel less alone."

We restructured her giving into something sustainable and intentional, but it opened my eyes to how emotional needs can drive financial decisions.

Sometimes it's spending to create temporary excitement with shopping sprees, excessive travel, and gifts because it fills the emptiness for a moment.

I've even seen people chase risky investments because money becomes a substitute for meaning.

BUILDING YOUR FOUNDATION BEFORE YOU NEED IT

So what can you do about this? You can start preparing now:

- **Reconnect before you need to.** Reach out to friends, neighbors, or colleagues you've lost touch with. Nurture work friendships outside the office before you retire;
- **Get involved in community.** Churches, service groups, and alumni associations. Many retirees find real purpose in giving back;
- **Find hobbies with people.** Golf leagues, book clubs, fitness classes. Is there a hobby or activity you used to do when you were younger?
- **Identify what energized you at work.** Mentoring? Problem-solving? Leading? Find places to use those skills in retirement.

After some conversation about these ideas, James realized what he missed most about his job was teaching. So he started volunteering with a local community college. He later told me, "That gave me back the sense of purpose I was afraid of losing."

The people I know who retire best often say, "I'm busier now than when I was working."

Ray's Rule #24
Don't just retire from something.
Retire to something.

ARE YOU REALLY READY?

Before you file your retirement paperwork, I want you to ask yourself these questions:

- How will I define myself after work ends?
- What will my typical day look like?
- Who will I spend time with once I'm not around coworkers?
- Do my spouse and I share the same vision for retirement?
- What steps am I taking now to stay physically active and mentally sharp?

Retirement is a major life transition, and without a plan for how you'll spend your time, it's easy to slip into boredom, isolation, or even regret.

THE BOTTOM LINE

You didn't save for decades just to be bored or lonely in retirement.

True retirement success means having both the financial security to cover your needs and the purpose to make your days meaningful.

> **Ray's Rule #25**
> Your plan isn't complete until your calendar is as resilient as your portfolio.

In the next chapter, we're going to talk about protecting your legacy. Because after watching hundreds of families navigate this transition, I can tell you that the difference between a legacy that blesses your family and one that burdens them often comes down to a few simple decisions made at the right time.

YOUR CHAPTER 8 CHECKPOINT

Take a moment to reflect on these questions:

1. Have you thought about what will give you purpose and structure in retirement, besides managing your money?
2. If you woke up tomorrow retired, who are three people you'd spend your day with, and what would you do?
3. Could a lack of connection or purpose tempt you into making poor financial decisions just to fill the void?

Mini Exercise

The 7-7-7 Purpose Map

1. **List seven people** you want in your weekly orbit (friends, family, mentors). Schedule contact with three this week.
2. **Pick seven activities** (move, make, learn, serve, play, create, explore). Block time for two this week.
3. **Choose seven places** you'll go (gym, trail, library, church, workshop, cafe, volunteer site). Put one on the calendar within the next five days.

CHAPTER 9

LEGACY LOST: HOW POOR PLANNING HURTS THE PEOPLE YOU LOVE MOST

THREE SIBLINGS, LAUREN, ERIC, and Monica, sat across from me, barely making eye contact. Their father, Thomas[25], had passed away with a clear will stating that everything should be split equally among them. But his largest IRA named only Monica as beneficiary.

The siblings were confused. Eric asked, "Why did Dad do this?" Monica was devastated, convinced her siblings thought she'd manipulated him.

But Thomas had been thoughtful. There was a good reason he did this. Monica was in a lower tax bracket than her siblings, which meant she'd pay less tax on the IRA distributions. In the end, their inheritance was fair to all three of his children, but their assets came from different places. But he never explained it to them. A thoughtful plan became a painful mystery.

Smart, successful people sometimes leave behind confusion and conflict, not because they didn't care, but because they didn't communicate.

In this chapter, we will cover how to avoid estate planning challenges that cost your family time and money, why your professionals need to be on the same page, and why the conversation you have with your children today might be the most valuable part of your legacy.

THE FIRST MISTAKE: THINKING YOUR WILL CONTROLS EVERYTHING

Most people believe their will controls their entire estate. It doesn't.

Contract-controlled assets, such as retirement accounts, life insurance, annuities, and bank accounts with transfer-on-death (TOD) or payable-on-death (POD) designations, pay out to whoever you named as beneficiary on each account, regardless of your will. The beneficiary form always wins. Always.

Patricia[26] learned this the hard way. Despite being married for over twenty years and having updated wills, she didn't inherit her husband's IRA. They had updated their wills, but they needed to make sure this was also reflected on the paperwork for the individual accounts. Since they didn't do this, the IRA still listed his ex-wife from a marriage that ended decades earlier.

Ray's Rule #26
Beneficiary designations outrank your will - every time.

THE SECOND MISTAKE: NEVER EXPLAINING YOUR PLAN

When beneficiary designations and the will don't match, and no one knows why, children fill in the blanks. "Wait a minute, what's going on here? Why am I not getting a third of the IRA?"

They are left to draw their own conclusions. And those conclusions often involve hurt feelings, assumptions about favoritism, and sometimes relationships that never fully recover. Thoughtful tax strategy ends up looking like favoritism without context.

THE THIRD MISTAKE: LEAVING YOUR FAMILY TO PLAY DETECTIVE

Remember Tina from Chapter 4, with her eight bank accounts across three towns? That confusion becomes a massive burden for your family when you're gone.

Without clear organization, your family faces probate delays, may discover accounts years later missing critical deadlines, and could spend thousands tracking down assets.

WHEN PROFESSIONALS DON'T COORDINATE

Even if you get your beneficiaries right, communicate with your family, and organize your accounts, everything can still fall apart when your professionals aren't in alignment.

I've seen families burn months in court and tens of thousands of dollars in fees because titles, beneficiaries, and tax strategy weren't synchronized.

HERE'S HOW TO FIX IT (AND GIVE CLARITY TO YOUR FAMILY)

Now that you understand the problems, let me show you how you can protect your family from them.

MATCH THE RIGHT ASSETS TO THE RIGHT PEOPLE OR ORGANIZATIONS

Not all inherited assets are taxed the same way, and understanding these differences can save your family tens of thousands of dollars.

Traditional retirement accounts (IRAs, 401(k)s) are fully taxable as ordinary income to whoever inherits them. Your children will pay tax on every dollar they withdraw, often at their highest rates during peak earning years.

Roth retirement accounts, by contrast, Roth IRAs provide unique tax characteristics that may be advantageous in some inheritance situations. Qualified distributions are generally income-tax-free under current law; however, beneficiaries remain subject to required distribution rules and potential estate-tax considerations.

Non-retirement assets, like your house, stocks in a taxable brokerage account, or other property, receive what's called a "step-up in cost basis." Here's what that means:

You bought stock for $100 per share. At your death, it's worth $200 per share. Your daughter inherits it and sells it at $205. She only pays capital gains tax on that $5 of growth after inheritance, not the $100 of growth during your lifetime.

That step-up applies to most property you own, including real estate, though the rules get complex with jointly-owned property. Always coordinate with your tax professional on property transfers.

One exception: Non-qualified annuities are purchased with after-tax money and they do not receive a step-up in cost basis at death. Instead, beneficiaries generally inherit the contract subject to *income-in-respect-of-a-decedent (IRD)* rules. Your original principal investment generally is not taxed again, but the growth is taxed as ordinary income to your heirs.

The bottom line: For some families engaged in legacy and estate planning, it may be advantageous to consider which assets are left to which beneficiaries.

In certain situations, tax-deferred retirement accounts are left to charities, who generally pay no income tax, or to heirs in lower tax brackets, while Roth accounts and assets that may receive a step-up in cost basis are left to other family members.

While the total value of the inheritance may be similar, the after-tax outcomes for beneficiaries can differ significantly depending on asset type, beneficiary tax status, and applicable rules.

These strategies are highly individualized and should be reviewed in coordination with qualified tax and estate-planning professionals.

USE LIFE INSURANCE THE SMART WAY

A well-sized life insurance death benefit may be used as part of an overall estate plan to help equalize inheritances or offset taxes created by Roth conversions or concentrated illiquid assets (family property). Just remember, keep the beneficiaries on your life insurance policy aligned with your plan.

Life insurance benefits are subject to policy provisions and the claims-paying ability of the issuing insurer. As with all planning strategies, coordination among beneficiary designations, account titling, and the broader financial plan is essential.

COORDINATE EVERYTHING ON PAPER

When I build a tax-efficient legacy plan with clients, we focus on three levers:

1. **Spend vs. Preserve** - Which accounts to spend in retirement and which accounts to leave for the next generation;
2. **Roth Strategy** - Using Roth conversions strategically, particularly in years when your tax bracket may be lower, to potentially improve the after-tax treatment of assets for heirs under current tax law (always in coordination with your tax professional);
3. **Designation Match** - Making sure beneficiary designations match your overall estate plan.

For complex wishes (timing, protection, special-needs children), your attorney may recommend trusts, and your financial advisor should ensure the funding/beneficiary details match the trust documents.

IT'S YOUR STORY TO TELL

All of these decisions are important, but if you're not telling your children the WHY behind them, they're going to draw their own conclusions. And those conclusions often lead to unnecessary hurt feelings.

If Thomas had simply sat down with Lauren, Eric, and Monica and explained, "Here's why I'm structuring the beneficiaries this way. Monica's in a lower tax bracket, which means she'll pay less tax on the IRA. But I'm balancing it out through other assets, so everyone gets about the same after taxes," that entire conflict could have been avoided. There would have been no mystery and no mistrust.

Here's what your children need from you:

- Your overall wishes
- How the inheritance is structured and why
- The tax implications of what they'll receive
- Who is in which role (Executor, Power of Attorney, Trustee) and why
- The intention behind your decisions
- Where to find the documents and contacts

It's your story. You should be the one telling it.

THREE THINGS YOU NEED TO DO RIGHT NOW

If you take nothing else from this chapter, do these three things:

1. REVIEW YOUR BENEFICIARIES TODAY

I mean **today.** Pull out every account statement, including retirement accounts, life insurance, and bank accounts with TOD designations, and check who's listed. Has anyone's name changed through marriage or divorce? Have you gotten remarried? Do the beneficiaries still match your current intentions? While you're at it, verify contingent beneficiaries, too.

This is the easiest and most important step in estate planning, and yet it's the one people skip most often.

2. GET YOUR TEAM TALKING

Call your financial advisor and ask, "When's the last time you talked to my CPA and my attorney about my overall plan?"

If the answer is "never," you've got a problem that needs fixing. Put a joint call on the calendar.

3. HAVE THE CONVERSATION

Call your children. Not someday. Not when things are "finalized." Now.

Explain your plan. Tell them why you made the choices you did. Give them clarity instead of leaving them to guess after you're gone.

The most important gift you can give your children isn't money but *clarity* about your intentions and the reasoning behind them.

THE BOTTOM LINE

You worked too hard to leave your family with confusion, conflict, or unnecessary taxes.

Leaving a real legacy means taking steps to pass on clarity, efficiency, and compassion and giving the right assets to the right people, documented and explained.

In the next chapter, we're going to step back and look at the question: "Do we have enough?" I hear this question all the time, and I have learned that the real answer isn't about hitting a magic number. It's about understanding what that number needs to do for you. Let me show you why the account balance everyone obsesses over might not be the number that matters most.

YOUR CHAPTER 9 CHECKPOINT

Take a moment to reflect on these questions:

1. If you passed away tomorrow, would your family inherit clarity or chaos?
2. Do your beneficiary forms, account titles, and will/trust all match?
3. Have you reviewed how taxes will affect what your heirs actually receive from your retirement accounts?

Mini-Exercise:

1. List every account; note the primary and contingent beneficiaries; highlight any that don't match with your will/trust.
2. Identify the primary tax characteristics of each asset (taxable, tax-deferred, or potentially tax-free) and evaluate how different asset types may be aligned with heirs or charitable beneficiaries to help improve after-tax outcomes, subject to applicable rules and individual circumstances.
3. Write a five-sentence "letter of intent" in plain English explaining the why. Save it with your documents, and send a copy to your executor.

CHAPTER 10

THE NUMBER THAT REALLY MATTERS: IT'S NOT HOW MUCH YOU HAVE; IT'S HOW MUCH YOU NEED

"Do We Have Enough?"

It's the question I hear more than any other.

Dennis asked it. Susan asked it. Just about everyone who sits across from me eventually asks it.

"How much do we need?" "Is our net worth enough?"

They're *really* asking, "Are we going to be okay?"

That's an honest and important question. The truth is the money you have saved isn't the number that matters most. It's a scorecard, not a plan.

Your real security doesn't come from how big the number on your balance sheet is. It comes from whether that number can create reliable income for as long as you live.

THE NUMBER YOU'LL NEVER KNOW

If we're being honest, the most important number in retirement is one we'll never know, and that is how old we'll be when we die.

That number drives everything. How long your savings must last, how much you can safely spend, and how you balance today's enjoyment with tomorrow's security.

The challenge is that we don't get to know that number in advance.

So we plan for the possibility that you'll live longer than you expect. Because living longer is a blessing . . . unless you run out of money while you're still healthy and active.

THE SECOND MOST IMPORTANT NUMBER

If we can't know how long you'll live, we turn to the second most important number: how much income you need to live the life you want.

This is where the real planning begins.

These are the things that make life *feel rich*, including travel, family gatherings, giving, hobbies, and the freedom to say "yes" without fear.

Once we know that income target, we can reverse-engineer the rest.

- How much of that income will come from predictable income sources (Social Security, pensions, annuities)?
- How much will come from variable sources (investments, rentals, part-time work)?
- What's the gap, and how do we fill it safely?

Ray's Rule #27

Net worth is what you have. Income is what you live on. Clarity comes from knowing the difference.

HOW "ENOUGH" REALLY WORKS

When clients first meet with me, many are fixated on hitting a certain milestone. "I want to get to $1 million." Or $2 million. Or $5 million. Like the number is some kind of trophy.

But a millionaire with no plan can still run out of money. Meanwhile, I've seen people with far less live with total confidence because they understood their income plan.

Here's how I explain it: Your portfolio isn't a medal. It's a tool. Its job is to create a lifetime paycheck that adjusts for changing needs, inflation, and taxes while protecting you from market surprises and the unknowns of aging.

When you can see where every dollar of your income will come from, and know it's built to last, that's when you can finally relax and enjoy what you've built.

THE THREE NUMBERS THAT DEFINE RETIREMENT SUCCESS

NUMBER	MEANING	WHY IT MATTERS
Longevity (the unknowable number)	How long you'll live	Drives every planning decision. The longer you live, the more income you'll need.
Income (the essential number)	What you'll need and how you'll generate it	Determines whether you can live freely or fearfully.
Net Worth (the supporting number)	What you've saved	It's not the finish line; it's the fuel that powers your income engine.

Ray's Rule #28

You don't win the game by dying with the biggest account — you win by living your best life.

We can't control longevity. We can define lifestyle. And we can absolutely improve income efficiency — by coordinating taxes, investment risk, and withdrawal strategy.

That's how we transform anxiety into assurance.

THE BOTTOM LINE

So when someone asks me, "Do we have enough?", here's what I tell them:

"I don't know yet. But I know how we'll find out. We're going to calculate exactly how much income you need, identify where it's coming from, and stress-test whether it'll last as long as you do. Then you'll know, not guess, not hope, but know, whether you're okay."

YOUR CHAPTER 10 CHECKPOINT

Take a moment to reflect on these questions:

1. Are you fixated on reaching a specific net worth milestone, or do you understand how much income that money needs to generate?
2. Do you know your monthly income gap, which is the difference between your guaranteed income sources and your actual spending needs?
3. When you think about retirement, are you more worried about your account balance or your monthly paycheck?

Mini-Exercise

Take out a notepad:

1. Write your expected monthly retirement income from predictable income sources (Social Security, pensions, annuities).
2. List your monthly spending (essentials + lifestyle + fun).
3. Subtract the two. That's your income gap.
4. Review where that gap will come from, including IRAs, brokerage, and cash flow, and ask, "Can I sustain this gap for thirty years without running out of money?"

If the answer feels uncertain, that's where your work begins.

CONCLUSION

FROM ANXIETY TO CONFIDENCE: YOUR RETIREMENT SUCCESS ROADMAP

LET'S REVISIT SARAH AND Jim from the introduction. I ran into Sarah at the grocery store about six months after we'd built their retirement plan together. Her whole face lit up.

"Ray, we're going to Colorado to see the grandkids, something we've been putting off for three years. And we're getting that new car." She paused. "It feels good to finally know we can."

That's what this book has been about. Not just having enough but knowing you have enough and having the confidence to actually live your best life.

Ray's Rule #29
Financial freedom isn't a dollar amount.
It's the peace of mind knowing you'll be okay,
no matter what happens next.

WHAT I'VE LEARNED

After working with hundreds of retirees just like you, I've learned five things that separate the anxious from the confident:

1. **Retirement is about more than money.** Having enough savings matters, but true success comes from having purpose, connection, and confidence in how your money supports your life;
2. **Coordination beats size.** I've seen $3 million households who worry and households with $800,000 who sleep well. The difference? Scattered accounts, disconnected professionals, and uncoordinated strategies cause more problems than not having "enough";
3. **Most people focus on the wrong number.** The amount you've saved isn't the magic number. What matters more than your total assets is whether your income sources can match your expenses throughout retirement. Net worth is a scorecard; income is a lifeline;
4. **Communication is key.** Spouses, children, and professionals must share the same story. Silence or assumptions usually lead to conflict, stress, and mistakes;
5. **Planning is ongoing.** Life changes. Laws change. Markets change. Retirement planning isn't something you set

> and forget. It's a living process that adapts with you. I was introduced to a couple who thought their plan was "done" ten years ago. When we revisited everything, their tax brackets had shifted, investments had drifted out of balance, and their estate documents no longer matched reality. We didn't tweak; we rebuilt. A one-time plan is like a snapshot. An ongoing relationship is like a GPS. It's constantly recalculating to keep you on course.

After reading about all these potential mistakes, you may feel overwhelmed. You might be thinking, "Oh no, I'm making half of these mistakes right now."

Don't panic.

Most of these mistakes are common, and they can be fixed.

When I meet with new clients, I ask them questions like these. Their answers tell me immediately where the gaps are:

- *Are you more focused on avoiding losses today than making sure your money lasts twenty to thirty years?*
- *Do you find yourself holding back on travel, hobbies, or experiences because you're afraid of "what if"?*
- *Have you thought about how much of your IRA or 401(k) really belongs to you versus what may be subject to IRS tax obligations?*
- *Are you juggling accounts instead of having one clear, simple picture of how your money works together?*
- *If something happened to you tomorrow, would your spouse know what you own and who to call?*
- *Do both of you understand how your retirement income will work?*

- *Do you have a strategy for when to file for Social Security that's based on analysis, or are you planning to just "start when you need it"?*
- *Have you thought about what will give you purpose and structure in retirement, beyond managing your money?*
- *If you passed away tomorrow, would your family inherit clarity or chaos?*
- *When you make a change in one area, like investments or estate documents, do you know how it affects the others?*

If even one question stings, you're not alone. And more importantly, you're exactly where you need to be. You're aware and ready to take action.

Awareness is the first win.

YOUR FIRST THREE STEPS

You don't have to fix everything overnight. Here's where to start:

Step 1: Get clarity. Make a simple list of your accounts, your income sources, and the professionals you rely on, including your tax professional, attorney, and financial advisor. Just putting everything in one place will give you a clearer picture than most people have.

Step 2: Prioritize. Ask yourself: What worries me most right now? Maybe it's taxes. Maybe it's when to file for Social Security. Maybe it's whether your spouse would know what to do if something happened to you. Start there. Address that first, then move on to the next.

Step 3: Build momentum. Fix one thing, then move on to the next. Each step reduces stress and builds confidence.

You don't have to do it alone. The biggest reason people stay stuck in these mistakes is that they keep guessing instead of getting coordinated advice. Look, you hired professionals because you wanted expert help. But having experts isn't enough if they're not talking to each other. It's like having the best offensive line in football, but nobody knows the play. Working with someone who can pull all the pieces together and ensure your team is synchronized will save you time, money, and stress.

Start small, get clarity, and then build a coordinated plan that puts you back in charge of your retirement.

ONCE YOU'VE TAKEN THOSE FIRST STEPS

Once people start getting clarity, they will often ask me, "How do I know when I'm truly ready to retire?"

Being ready for retirement has two sides. **Financial and emotional**. Both have to be in place before you can step away with confidence.

On the **financial** side, you're ready when you have reliable income sources covering your essential expenses. You know how much you can safely spend without running out. Your tax strategy, estate plan, and healthcare costs are built into the plan.

On the **emotional** side, you're ready when you have a vision for how you'll spend your days, not just the first year, but the next twenty or thirty. You feel a sense of purpose and connection outside of work. You and your spouse are on the same page about what retirement will look like.

You're truly ready for retirement when the numbers work, and your heart is at peace. This means having clarity, purpose, and confidence in the next chapter of your life.

SO WHAT DOES THIS MEAN FOR YOU?

It means you've spent forty-plus years getting to this point in your life. You're not going to put together your plan for the next twenty-plus years in just one day, one week, or even one month.

It will be an ongoing process.

But you have to start.

That's really the critical decision. "Do I start on my retirement plan now or wait?"

Look, retirement planning can feel like drinking from a firehose with all of the accounts, taxes, Social Security, and estate planning. It's too much if you tackle it all at once.

We need to take it step by step. Turn many streams into one steady flow you can drink from. Clarity and coordination can turn overwhelm into confidence.

ONE LAST THING BEFORE YOU GO

Retirement success doesn't happen by accident. It's not about guessing, hoping, or waiting until "someday." It's about taking control by making intentional choices that are designed to protect your income, reduce your taxes, and give you confidence that all the pieces of your financial life actually work together.

My message is simple. You've worked hard to build what you have, and thoughtful planning can help bring greater confidence and clarity to how those resources support your life today and your goals for the future.

By coordinating strategies with the right guidance, many families seek a clearer path toward enjoying the present, preparing for what lies ahead, and thoughtfully providing for the people who matter most.

Retirement planning often involves many moving parts and managing them alone can feel overwhelming. With professional guidance, those complexities can be addressed within a coordinated planning process, allowing you to focus more fully on the people and activities that matter most to you.

My goal is to support informed decision-making and provide clarity as your needs and priorities evolve.

Take control of your retirement, and turn it into the most rewarding chapter of your life.

RESOURCES

FIVE QUESTIONS TO ASK YOURSELF

Let me give you five questions I ask every new client. If you can't answer these confidently, you've got gaps.

Does each account have a job? Every account should fall into income (now), growth (later), or legacy (never). If you're not sure which is which, things aren't coordinated.

Have your professionals talked recently? If your financial advisor, CPA, and attorney have never spoken about your overall plan, you have gaps.

Do your documents and beneficiaries match? Your will, trust, and account beneficiaries should tell the same story.

Are taxes part of the plan? If your strategy only looks at investments and ignores withdrawal orders, RMDs, Roth strategies, or how Social Security affects taxes, it's incomplete.

Do you have clarity and confidence? If you're unsure how your money works together, or you're second-guessing decisions, coordination is missing.

When everything's coordinated, your accounts, professionals, documents, taxes, and goals all work together. If even one is out of sync, you don't have a complete plan.

THE FAMILY FINANCIAL CONVERSATION SCRIPT

Title: *"We Love You, and We Need to Talk About Money."*

1. OPENING THE DOOR (EMPATHY FIRST)

"We love you, and we want to see you succeed. You know we've always tried to be there for you when you've needed help. As we're planning our own retirement, we need to make sure that what we do financially helps you but doesn't put our future at risk."

Goal: Start from love, not guilt. Make the conversation about shared responsibility, not blame.

2. EXPLAIN THE BIG PICTURE (TRANSPARENCY WITHOUT DETAILS)

"We've built a financial plan for our retirement, including our income, healthcare, and long-term needs. That plan has limits, and we have to stay within them, so we don't become a financial burden later. That's why we need to talk about what kind of help is realistic and what isn't."

Tip: Use phrases like *"our plan," "what we can responsibly do,"* and *"we've looked at the numbers."* It shows this isn't about emotion; it's about stewardship.

3. DEFINE THE BOUNDARIES (KIND BUT CLEAR)

"Here's what we can do: we can help with [specific, limited support. e.g., a one-time payment, matching contribution, or set monthly amount]. What we can't do is ongoing or open-ended support."

"We're happy to talk about ways to help you build stability, but we can't compromise our own."

- One-time help: "We'll cover X once."
- Conditional help: "We'll match your payments for Y months."
- No: "We can't keep paying rent or credit cards."

4. SHIFT TOWARD EMPOWERMENT (ENCOURAGE OWNERSHIP)

"You're capable. We believe in you. Our support should help you move forward, not hold you back. Let's talk about what steps you can take to strengthen your finances over the next few months."

Tip: Ask open questions:

- "What's your plan for covering this after our support ends?"
- "What would make you feel more independent long-term?"

5. CLOSE WITH LOVE AND UNITY

"We aren't having this conversation to pull away. We're protecting our relationship. We want to be there for family moments, not financial crises. We love you, and we'll always be in your corner."

Follow-Up

- **Optional Written Agreement:** A short email confirming what was discussed helps avoid confusion later.
- **Check-In:** Revisit after sixty or ninety days to celebrate progress or adjust expectations.

RAY'S RULES

Ray's Rule #1

Safety isn't a steady account value.
Safety is steady purchasing power.

Ray's Rule #2

The biggest risk isn't a bad market year. It's a bad sequence of expenses when you're unprepared.

Ray's Rule #3

Lead with capacity. Let tolerance influence the mix, but never overrule the math.

Ray's Rule #4

Money without an assignment will default to anxiety. Give every dollar a job.

Ray's Rule #5

Money can buy freedom, but it cannot buy back time.

Ray's Rule #6

Clarity creates confidence; confidence unlocks experiences.

Ray's Rule #7

In retirement, the hardest check to write is the one to yourself.

Ray's Rule #8

Front-load joy while you have the health to enjoy it.

Ray's Rule #9

Reclaim what's rightfully yours by making sure the IRS gets only what it's owed, not a penny more.

Ray's Rule #10

The time to protect your spouse from the widow's tax trap is while you're both still here.

Ray's Rule #11

If you wait until the IRS tells you what to withdraw, or let them determine the amount you need to withdraw, you're not in control; the government is.

Ray's Rule #12

You can't control the laws that Congress passes, but you can control how prepared your family is.

Ray's Rule #13

Simplicity is good; synchronization is better.

Ray's Rule #14

Your plan is only as strong as its weakest link.

Ray's Rule #15

Social Security is not a form that you file, but is a foundation that you optimize.

Ray's Rule #16

The right filing age depends on your income mix, not your neighbor's birthday.

Ray's Rule #17

When you file, you're choosing your spouse's survivor check as much as your own.

Ray's Rule #18

A good plan fails if only one person knows it.

Ray's Rule #19

Clarity now prevents conflict later.

Ray's Rule #20

A bailout without behavior change is an invitation to repeat the crisis.

Ray's Rule #21

This isn't about being selfish! Give them a ladder to climb. Don't carry them over the wall.

Ray's Rule #22

A plan can't solve every emotion, but it can remove financial ambiguity so you can lead with love and limits.

Ray's Rule #23

Money funds retirement. Meaning fills it.

Ray's Rule #24

Don't just retire from something. Retire to something.

Ray's Rule #25

Your plan isn't complete until your calendar is as resilient as your portfolio.

Ray's Rule #26

Beneficiary designations outrank your will every time.

Ray's Rule #27

Net worth is what you have. Income is what you live on. Clarity comes from knowing the difference.

Ray's Rule #28

You don't win the game by dying with the biggest account. You win by living your best life.

Ray's Rule #29

Financial freedom isn't a dollar amount. It's the peace of mind knowing you'll be okay, no matter what happens next.

ESSENTIAL EXPENSES CHECKLIST

List of essential expenses that should be covered by guaranteed income:

- Food
- Housing
- Transportation
- Utilities
- Healthcare/Insurance

Category	**Monthly Estimate**	**Predictable Income Source (Social Security / defined benefit Pension / Annuity)**	**Covered? (Y/N)**
Housing			
Food			
Transportation			
Health and Insurance			
Utilities			

RETIREMENT PLAN COORDINATION WORKSHEET[27]

Instructions: Assign an owner, set a target date, and check done when completed.

TEAM AND DOCUMENTS

TASK	OWNER	TARGET DATE	DONE	NOTES
Confirm advisor/planner is quarterback for coordination.			☐	
Confirm CPA/ tax professional contact information.			☐	
Confirm estate attorney contact information.			☐	
List trusted contact(s) for emergencies.			☐	
List where key documents are stored (secure folder/location).			☐	

INCOME SOURCES

TASK	OWNER	TARGET DATE	DONE	NOTES
Social Security plan documented (start age and estimated benefit).			☐	
Pension election reviewed (options and survivorship).			☐	
Other income sources documented (rental, part-time, etc.).			☐	
Create paycheck replacement schedule (transfers/bill pay).			☐	

ACCOUNTS AND ASSETS

TASK	OWNER	TARGET DATE	DONE	NOTES
Inventory all retirement accounts (401(k)/403(b) /IRA/Roth).			☐	
Inventory taxable accounts and bank accounts.			☐	
Inventory CDs/ treasuries/ bonds and maturity dates.			☐	
Inventory annuities/ insurance contracts (fees/ surrender/ benefits).			☐	
Inventory real estate and business interests (if applicable).			☐	

BENEFICIARIES AND TITLING

TASK	OWNER	TARGET DATE	DONE	NOTES
Review beneficiaries on every account (primary and contingent).			☐	
Confirm account titling matches estate plan (TOD/JTWROS/trust).			☐	
Update outdated beneficiaries, addresses, and contact info.			☐	

RISK AND DOWNTURN PLAN

TASK	OWNER	TARGET DATE	DONE	NOTES
Confirm risk capacity (time horizon, flexibility, required return).			☐	
Set liquidity target for 0-24 months of planned spending.			☐	
Document bad-year plan (spending, withdrawals, rebalancing).			☐	
Identify and address concentration risks (single stock/ employer).			☐	

TAX AND WITHDRAWALS

TASK	OWNER	TARGET DATE	DONE	NOTES
Confirm RMD timeline and first distribution year.			☐	
Set withholding/estimated tax plan for SS/pension/IRA.			☐	
Evaluate Roth conversions (timing and bracket targets).			☐	
Document withdrawal order (taxable/pre-tax/Roth) and guardrails.			☐	
Consider charitable tax strategies (QCD if eligible).			☐	

HEALTHCARE AND PROTECTION

TASK	OWNER	TARGET DATE	DONE	NOTES
Medicare plan selected (A/B + Medigap/ Advantage + Part D).			☐	
HSA strategy coordinated (stop contributions timing if needed).			☐	
Long-term care plan discussed (self-fund/ coverage options).			☐	
Review umbrella and property/ liability coverage limits.			☐	

IMPLEMENTATION AND REVIEW

TASK	OWNER	TARGET DATE	DONE	NOTES
Track transfers/ rollovers and confirm completion in writing			☐	
Capture cost basis for taxable holdings.			☐	
Schedule annual review and Q3/ Q4 tax check-in.			☐	
Update plan after any life change (health, move, inheritance, etc.).			☐	

NOTES / FOLLOW-UPS:

IMPORTANT DOCUMENTS LOCATION LIST

HOUSEHOLD INFORMATION

Primary household name		**Spouse/ partner (optional)**	
Date completed		**Next review due**	
Prepared by		**Trusted contact**	

How to use this list: Write where each document lives (physical + digital), who has access, and when it was last updated. Keep this list in a safe place and review at least annually—or after major life changes.

PRIMARY STORAGE LOCATIONS (FILL IN YOUR "GO-TO" PLACES)

CATEGORY	PHYSICAL LOCATION	DIGITAL LOCATION / LINK	WHO HAS ACCESS?
Home file cabinet (folder name)			
Fireproof safe (location/combination holder)			
Safe deposit box (bank/branch/ box #)			
Attorney (originals held)			
Planner/Advisor (copies held)			
Cloud storage (Drive/Dropbox/ OneDrive)			
Password manager / vault			

DOCUMENT INVENTORY (WHAT IT IS + WHERE IT LIVES)

TASK	OWNER	TARGET DATE	DONE	NOTES
Will / Codicil			☐	
Trust documents (if applicable)			☐	
Power of Attorney (financial)			☐	
Healthcare Proxy / Living Will			☐	
HIPAA authorization			☐	
Beneficiary confirmations (latest)			☐	
Life insurance policies			☐	
Annuity contracts			☐	
Property deed(s)			☐	
Mortgage / HELOC documents			☐	
Vehicle titles			☐	

Use this page for additional documents and your emergency access plan.

ADDITIONAL DOCUMENTS (FINANCIAL, TAX, IDENTITY, AND LEGACY)

DOCUMENT TYPE	PHYSICAL LOCATION	DIGITAL LOCATION	OWNER / ACCOUNT / REF #	LAST UPDATED
Social Security cards / IDs / Passports				
Birth / marriage / divorce certificates				
Military/DD214 (if applicable)				
Tax returns (last 3–7 years) + key supporting docs				
Estate/tax filings (if applicable)				
Retirement plan statements (401k/IRA) - latest				
Brokerage statements - latest				

Bank account list + statements - latest				
Social Security / pension award letters				
Medicare card + supplemental policy info				
Long-term care policy (if applicable)				
Business documents / ownership agreements (if applicable)				
Funeral/burial wishes or prepaid plan				
Digital assets list (accounts, photos, subscriptions)				

EMERGENCY ACCESS PLAN (WHO TO CALL + WHAT TO SHARE)

1) First call (name/relationship/phone):__________________

2) Attorney (name/phone): ______________________________

3) CPA/Tax Pro (name/phone): __________________________

4) Financial Planner/Advisor (name/phone): ______________

What can be shared and with whom?

____

NOTES

____

____

____

____

____

____

BENEFICIARY REVIEW CHECKLIST

Important: Beneficiary forms often override your will/trust for retirement accounts, life insurance, and accounts with POD/TOD. Always confirm updates in writing and store confirmations with your estate documents.

A) ACCOUNTS & POLICIES TO REVIEW (CHECK EACH ITEM THAT EXISTS)

ITEM	EXISTS	PRIMARY CONFIRMED	CONTINGENT CONFIRMED	NOTES
Employer plan(s): 401(k) / 403(b) / 457 / TSP	☐	☐	☐	
Traditional IRA(s)	☐	☐	☐	
Roth IRA(s)	☐	☐	☐	
Annuity contract(s)	☐	☐	☐	
Life insurance policy(ies) (term/ permanent)	☐	☐	☐	
Bank accounts w/ POD (checking/ savings/MM)	☐	☐	☐	
Brokerage accounts w/ TOD	☐	☐	☐	
HSA	☐	☐	☐	
529 / education account (successor owner/ beneficiary)	☐	☐	☐	
Other (describe):	☐	☐	☐	

B) BENEFICIARY DETAILS CHECKLIST (CATCH COMMON MISTAKES)

CHECK	DONE	NOTES
Names match legal ID (spelling, middle initials, suffixes)	☐	
DOB and SSN/Tax ID added where allowed (reduces claim delays)	☐	
Addresses/phones updated (where forms allow)	☐	
Primary and contingent beneficiaries both listed	☐	
Percentages add to 100 percent (or correct per policy rules)	☐	
Per stirpes / per capita selection matches your intent	☐	
Minors are handled properly (guardian/trust/custodian plan in place)	☐	
Special needs planning considered (SNT/appropriate structure if needed)	☐	
No outdated beneficiaries (ex-spouse, deceased relatives, prior relationships)	☐	
No "blank contingent" risk where it matters	☐	

Use this page to confirm coordination, tax considerations, and follow-through.

C) COORDINATION WITH YOUR ESTATE PLAN

COORDINATION ITEM	DONE	NOTES
Your will/trust is current and reflects your beneficiary intent	☐	
Trust is named correctly (exact legal name, date) where applicable	☐	
Successor trustees/executors align with your plan	☐	
Powers of Attorney and Healthcare Proxy are current	☐	
Your account titling matches your intent (JTWROS / TOD / trust ownership)	☐	
Charitable gifts (if any) are documented correctly (beneficiary/QCD plan)	☐	
If you moved states, forms and estate docs were reviewed for your new state	☐	

D) TAX & PLANNING CONSIDERATIONS (RETIREMENT ACCOUNTS & INSURANCE)

CONSIDERATION	REVIEWED	NOTES
Spousal vs non-spousal beneficiary implications discussed (IRAs/401k)	☐	
Roth vs pre-tax inheritance impact considered	☐	
Multiple beneficiaries—separate inherited accounts/tracking plan discussed	☐	
Insurance proceeds and intended use (income replacement, debt payoff, legacy)	☐	
Equalization plan discussed (if leaving different asset types to heirs)	☐	

E) DOCUMENTATION & FOLLOW-THROUGH

TASK	DONE	NOTES
Updated forms submitted (date):	☐	
Confirmation received and saved (screenshot/letter)	☐	
Copies stored with estate documents (location):	☐	
Trusted contact updated (where available)	☐	
Next annual review scheduled	☐	

Review triggers (do not wait for the annual meeting): Marriage/divorce, birth/adoption, death in the family, major inheritance/windfall, new account/policy, moving to a new state, changes in relationships, or a change in your estate documents.

NOTES

____

____

____

CASH FLOW ANALYSIS WORKSHEET

Use these pages for obligations, annual items, and your summary.

A) MONTHLY INCOME

INCOME SOURCE	GROSS	TAXES/ WITHHOLDING	NET (TAKE-HOME)	NOTES
Wages / self-employment				
Pension				
Social Security				
Rental income				
Dividends/ interest				
Other (describe)				
TOTAL MONTHLY INCOME				

B) ESSENTIAL MONTHLY EXPENSES (NEEDS)

CATEGORY	AMOUNT	NOTES/VENDOR
Housing (rent/mortgage)		
Property taxes / HOA		
Utilities (electric/gas/ water)		
Phone / internet		
Groceries		
Transportation (fuel/ maintenance)		
Auto insurance		
Homeowners/renters insurance		
Health insurance premiums		
Medical out-of-pocket		
Other essential (describe)		
TOTAL ESSENTIAL EXPENSES		

C) LIFESTYLE & DISCRETIONARY MONTHLY EXPENSES (WANTS)

CATEGORY	AMOUNT	NOTES
Dining out / entertainment		
Travel (monthly set-aside)		
Subscriptions / memberships		
Gifts / giving		
Hobbies		
Other discretionary (describe)		
TOTAL DISCRETIONARY EXPENSES		

D) DEBT & OBLIGATIONS (MONTHLY PAYMENTS)

DEBT/ OBLIGATION	MONTHLY PAYMENT	BALANCE (OPT.)	RATE (OPT.)	NOTES
Credit card(s)				
Auto loan				
Personal loan				
Student loan				
Other (describe)				
TOTAL DEBT PAYMENTS				

E) IRREGULAR / ANNUAL EXPENSES (MONTHLY EQUIVALENT)

ITEM	ANNUAL AMOUNT	MONTHLY EQUIVALENT	DUE MONTH (S)	NOTES
Income taxes (if not withheld)				
Home repairs / maintenance				
Auto repairs / replacement fund				
Other (describe)				
TOTAL ANNUAL ITEMS (MONTHLY EQ.)				

F) MONTHLY SUMMARY

Total monthly income (net): $______________________________

Total monthly expenses (B + C + D + E): $____________________

Monthly surplus / (deficit): $______________________________

If deficit, funding plan: ____________________________________

G) ACTION ITEMS

1. ____

2. ____

3. ____

NOTES

____

____

____

RETIREMENT READINESS SELF-ASSESSMENT (NON-FINANCIAL)

How Ready Are You . . . Really?

Money is only one part of a successful retirement. This assessment helps you evaluate your emotional, social, and lifestyle readiness so you can retire to something, not just from something.

1. IDENTITY AND PURPOSE

Rate each statement on a scale of 1 to 5

(1 = Not at all true, 5 = Completely true)

STATEMENT	1	2	3	4	5
I have a clear sense of purpose for this next chapter of life.					
I can describe how I'll spend my days in retirement (beyond "relaxing").					
I have activities that challenge me mentally and keep me engaged.					
I feel confident about who I am without my professional title or work identity.					

2. RELATIONSHIPS AND CONNECTION

STATEMENT	1	2	3	4	5
I have a strong network of friends or community groups I plan to stay involved with.					
I have shared retirement expectations with my spouse or partner.					
I have friends outside of work I spend time with regularly.					
I plan to maintain or grow my social connections after leaving work.					

3. HEALTH AND WELL-BEING

STATEMENT	1	2	3	4	5
I'm physically active and have a plan to maintain my health.					
I'm proactive about healthcare and preventive habits.					
I've thought about how I'll handle potential health changes or caregiving needs.					
I'm as intentional about my physical wellness as I am about my finances.					

4. COMMUNITY AND CONTRIBUTION

STATEMENT	1	2	3	4	5
I have causes, organizations, or volunteer work that give me a sense of contribution.					
I've considered how to use my professional skills or experience to give back.					
I'm excited about opportunities to make an impact outside of work.					

5. LIFESTYLE AND STRUCTURE

STATEMENT	1	2	3	4	5
I've thought about what a typical weekday will look like in retirement.					
I have a balance of rest, recreation, and routine planned.					
My spouse or partner and I share similar expectations about time together vs. independence.					
I've planned ways to keep learning, growing, or exploring new interests.					

SCORING AND REFLECTION

- **0 to 40 points:** You may be financially ready but not yet emotionally ready. Let's work together to define your next chapter with purpose.
- **41 to 70 points:** You have some clarity and confidence, but there are areas to refine before fully stepping away from work.
- **71 to 100 points:** You're well-positioned to retire to something meaningful. You've built purpose, structure, and connection into your plan.

PRE-RETIREMENT PLANNING TIMELINE WORKSHEET

Your Roadmap to a Confident and Coordinated Retirement

This worksheet helps you track the major milestones and decisions leading up to and immediately following your retirement. Use it to prepare, prioritize, and make each step intentional.

1. FIVE OR MORE YEARS BEFORE RETIREMENT: FOUNDATION AND VISION

- Clarify your vision for retirement, including lifestyle, location, family, purpose, and priorities.
- Estimate your retirement income needs (Essentials, Lifestyle, and Legacy categories).
- Review your current savings and projected growth.
- Evaluate your debt. Aim to eliminate or reduce major obligations before retirement.
- Check Social Security statements for accuracy and benefit estimates.
- Review your pension or employer plan options.
- Consider healthcare options and potential long-term care needs.
- Begin exploring tax-diversification strategies (Roth conversions, after-tax savings).
- Meet with a financial planner to model early retirement vs. full retirement age scenarios.
- Create or update your will, powers of attorney, and beneficiary designations.

NOTES:

____

____

____

2. TWO TO THREE YEARS BEFORE RETIREMENT: PREPARATION AND TESTING

- Update your detailed retirement budget. Compare projected income and expenses.
- Identify income gaps and strategies to fill them (annuities, part-time work, etc.).
- Review your investment allocation. Begin shifting toward income and risk management.
- Evaluate your home situation. Stay, downsize, or relocate?
- Explore healthcare options (Medicare, employer coverage, private plans).
- Begin Social Security filing analysis to determine your optimal start date.
- Review pension payout options and survivor benefits.
- Conduct a preliminary tax projection for the first retirement years.
- Revisit estate planning documents and insurance coverage.

NOTES:

3. ONE YEAR BEFORE RETIREMENT: COORDINATION AND IMPLEMENTATION

- Finalize your retirement date and confirm eligibility for employer benefits.
- Establish your income buckets: Now (0 to 5 years), Later (6 to 15 years), Legacy & Late-Stage (16 years and beyond).
- Consolidate and organize accounts to simplify management.
- Decide when and how you'll claim Social Security.
- Estimate first-year retirement income sources and taxes.
- Review healthcare transition plans (COBRA, Medicare, supplements).
- Schedule final meetings with your advisor, CPA, and attorney for coordination.
- Prepare a cash reserve for the first six to twelve months of living expenses.
- Discuss transition plans and emotional readiness with your spouse/partner.

NOTES:

4. AT RETIREMENT: TRANSITION AND ACTIVATION

- Execute rollover or transfer paperwork for employer accounts.
- Begin income distributions per your retirement income plan.
- Review withholding and estimated tax payments.
- Verify Social Security or pension payments have begun correctly.
- Enroll in Medicare (Parts A, B, D, and supplements).
- Reconfirm insurance coverage and beneficiary information.
- Create a master "Where Things Are" document for your spouse/family.
- Celebrate your retirement milestone. Plan your first intentional "retirement experience."

NOTES:

5. THE FIRST YEAR OF RETIREMENT: ADJUSTMENT AND REFINEMENT

- Review spending patterns and compare them to your plan.
- Adjust your withdrawal strategy if needed.
- Revisit your tax strategy. Explore bracket management and Roth opportunities.
- Evaluate how you're spending your time. Find purpose and routine.
- Meet with your advisor to review your first year and plan your next steps.
- Update estate documents, passwords, and contacts as needed.
- Reflect on lessons learned and set goals for year two.

NOTES:

YOUR NEXT STEP

Use this worksheet with your financial planner to ensure every decision is coordinated across taxes, investments, income, and estate planning. A confident retirement requires preparation, coordination, and clarity.

SOCIAL SECURITY FILING QUESTIONNAIRE

Key Questions to Ask Before You File

Filing for Social Security is one of the most important (and permanent) retirement decisions you'll ever make. Before you file, take a few minutes to reflect on these questions. Your answers will help you determine your best filing strategy, not just the earliest one.

1. PERSONAL AND HEALTH FACTORS

QUESTION	YOUR NOTES
What is your current age and your full retirement age (FRA)?	
How is your health today, and what is your family's longevity history?	
Have you had any recent changes in health, employment, or marital status?	
Do you expect to continue working after filing for benefits?	
If yes, what will your expected annual income be? (Earnings above certain limits may reduce early benefits.)	

2. SPOUSAL AND SURVIVOR CONSIDERATIONS

QUESTION	YOUR NOTES
Are you currently married, widowed, or divorced?	
What is your spouse's (or ex-spouse's) benefit amount or work record?	
Who has the higher benefit amount between you and your spouse?	
If one of you passed away first, how would that affect your household income?	
Have you discussed survivor benefits and which filing age protects the surviving spouse best?	

3. INCOME AND CASH FLOW NEEDS

QUESTION	YOUR NOTES
How much monthly income do you need to maintain your lifestyle?	
What other guaranteed income sources do you have (pension, annuity, etc.)?	
How much of your retirement income will depend on investment withdrawals?	
Could delaying Social Security allow your investments to grow or reduce withdrawals from taxable accounts?	

4. TAX COORDINATION

QUESTION	YOUR NOTES
Do you understand that up to 85 percent of your benefits may be taxable depending on your income?	
Have you reviewed how your IRA/401(k) withdrawals interact with Social Security taxation?	
Have you explored Roth conversions or tax-efficient withdrawal strategies before claiming?	
Do you plan to claim before or after Required Minimum Distributions begin?	

5. FILING TIMING AND BREAK-EVEN

QUESTION	YOUR NOTES
Do you know how much your benefit increases each year you delay beyond age sixty-two?	
Have you calculated your break-even age (when total delayed benefits exceed early benefits)?	
How long do you expect to live based on your health and family history?	
How would filing early versus delaying affect your surviving spouse's long-term security?	
Have you considered how inflation adjustments impact lifetime income?	

6. COORDINATION WITH YOUR OVERALL PLAN

QUESTION	YOUR NOTES
Have you coordinated your Social Security strategy with your overall income plan?	
Does your plan include a transition strategy? What income sources you'll use while waiting to file?	
Have you reviewed your filing decision with your financial advisor and tax professional together?	

ACCOUNT ORGANIZATION WORKSHEET

Clarify the Purpose of Every Dollar You Own

Use this worksheet to organize your accounts by purpose and time horizon, not just by where they're held. This helps ensure that every dollar you've saved is working in harmony with your financial plan.

1. INCOME ACCOUNTS: "NOW" (0 TO 5 YEARS)

Purpose: To fund your immediate income needs and protect against market downturns. Think: stability, access, and predictability.

ACCOUNT TYPE	INSTITUTION	CURRENT BALANCE	PURPOSE / EXPENSE IT COVERS	LIQUIDITY HIGH / MEDIUM / LOW

NOTES

2. GROWTH ACCOUNTS: "LATER" (6 TO 20 YEARS)

Purpose: To outpace inflation and refill your Income Accounts over time. Think: balance between protection and opportunity.

ACCOUNT TYPE	INSTITUTION	CURRENT BALANCE	INVEST-MENT OBJECTIVE	TIME HORIZON

NOTES

3. LEGACY ACCOUNTS: "NEVER" (NEXT GENERATION)

Purpose: To preserve wealth for heirs or charitable giving. Think: growth, tax-efficiency, and simplicity for your family.

ACCOUNT TYPE	INSTITUTION	CURRENT BALANCE	BENEFICIARY	TAX TYPE ROTH / TAXABLE / IRA

NOTES

REFILL FLOW SUMMARY

Later → Soon → Now

Use growth from Later Accounts to refill Income Accounts every few years. This keeps your plan flexible and your lifestyle steady, regardless of market swings.

ACTION STEPS

- ✓ Review each account and assign it a purpose.
- ✓ Verify beneficiaries and titles match your estate plan.
- ✓ Note any overlaps or inefficiencies.
- ✓ Review with your advisor annually to rebalance your "time buckets."

ABOUT THE AUTHOR

Ray Offenburger is a Certified Financial Planner®, specializing in retirement planning for professionals and their families. Unlike financial advisors who chase high returns or pressure quick decisions, Ray has built his practice on a patient, collaborative approach that prioritizes coordination over consolidation and ongoing relationships over transactions.

Ray's unique philosophy emerged from working extensively with retirees who had done everything "right" financially, maxing out 401(k)s, living below their means, accumulating substantial nest eggs, yet still felt anxious and overwhelmed as they approached or entered retirement. Through hundreds of client relationships, he discovered that successful retirement requires more than just reaching a magic number. It demands both "the financial security to sleep well at night and a reason to wake up in the morning."

His approach centers on risk capacity rather than risk tolerance, helping clients understand what their money actually needs to accomplish rather than what they think they can emotionally handle. Ray emphasizes the critical importance of coordination between scattered accounts, professional advisors, and family members, bringing together the financial, tax, estate, and personal elements that traditional retirement planning often treats as separate concerns.

A graduate of Seton Hall University and former educator, Ray brings a teacher's patience and clarity to complex financial concepts. He resides in Ocean County, NJ, with his wife,

Meredith, and their two sons, RJ and Christopher. When not helping clients navigate their retirement transitions, Ray can be found volunteering with the Sons of the American Legion and the Knights of Columbus. As a longtime New York Knicks fan, Ray has learned valuable lessons about optimism, patience, and long-term commitment, qualities that serve his clients well as they plan for retirement journeys that may span three decades or more.

ENDNOTES

1. The client names and stories in this book are composites. Names and identifying details have been changed or combined to protect client privacy. Any resemblance to specific individuals is coincidental.

2. This example is for illustrative purposes only.

3. Time-weighted asset allocation is a method of diversification that positions assets among major investment categories. This strategy may be used in an effort to manage risk and enhance returns but does not guarantee a profit or protect against loss in a declining market.

4. To safeguard the confidentiality of actual clients, names and identifying information have been modified.

5. To safeguard the confidentiality of actual clients, names and identifying information have been modified.

6. To safeguard the confidentiality of actual clients, names and identifying information have been modified.

7. This is a fictional couple created by using real scenarios from actual clients, names and identifying information have been modified.

8. This discussion is not intended to be tax advice. You should contact your tax professional to discuss your particular circumstances.

9. To safeguard the confidentiality of actual clients, names and identifying information have been modified.

10. Diversification cannot assure profit or guarantee against loss in a declining market

11. Diversification does not guarantee a profit or protect against loss in declining markets.

12. This is a sample for illustrative purposes only.

13. To safeguard the confidentiality of actual clients, names and identifying information have been modified.

14. This is a fictional couple created by using real scenarios from actual clients, names and identifying information have been modified

15. This is a fictional couple created by using real scenarios from actual clients, names and identifying information have been modified.

16. To safeguard the confidentiality of actual clients, names and identifying information have been modified.

17. To safeguard the confidentiality of actual clients, names and identifying information have been modified.

18. This is a fictional couple created by using real scenarios from actual clients; names and identifying information have been modified.

19. This is a fictional person created by using real scenarios from actual clients; names and identifying information have been modified.

20. To safeguard the confidentiality of actual clients, names and identifying information have been modified.

21. To safeguard the confidentiality of actual clients, names and identifying information have been modified.

22. To safeguard the confidentiality of actual clients, names and identifying information have been modified.

23. To safeguard the confidentiality of actual clients, names and identifying information have been modified.

24. To safeguard the confidentiality of actual clients, names and identifying information have been modified.

25. To safeguard the confidentiality of actual clients, names and identifying information have been modified.

26. To safeguard the confidentiality of actual clients, names and identifying information have been modified.

27. This information is intended to be educational and is not tailored to the investment needs of any specific investor.

www.ingramcontent.com/pod-product-compliance
Lightning Source LLC
LaVergne TN
LVHW022215200926
848481LV00006B/1973
* 9 7 9 8 9 5 0 5 8 3 1 4 8 *